PSALMS

A SELF-STUDY GUIDE

Irving L. Jensen

MOODY PRESS

CHICAGO

© 1968 by
THE MOODY BIBLE INSTITUTE
OF CHICAGO

Moody Press Revised Edition, 1990

Scripture quotations, unless noted otherwise, are taken from the King James Version.

The use of selected references from various versions of the Bible in this publication does not necessarily imply publisher endorsement of the version in its entirety.

ISBN: 0-8024-4463-6

5 7 9 10 8 6

Printed in the United States of America

CONTENTS

	Introduction	4
	The Book of Psalms	7
1	Psalms 1-10	17
2	Psalms 11-21	31
3	Psalms 22-30	43
4	Psalms 31-41	52
5	Psalms 42-55	64
6	Psalms 56-72	77
7	Psalms 73-89	93
8	Psalms 90-106	111
9	Psalms 107-119	124
10	Psalms 120-134	130
11	Psalms 135-150	135
	Bibliography	139

Introduction

The *book of Psalms* is perhaps the most widely read and quoted book of the Bible. But not many people tarry long enough in this book to seriously *study* its one hundred fifty chapters. This study guide has been prepared with the hope that it may encourage the reader to make a diligent and thorough examination of this inspired book. A major purpose of the many study questions of this manual is to put greater emphasis on the student's seeing for himself what the psalms are saying. This independent Bible study method is the approach emphasized by this writer in the other books of this self-study series. For further description of this inductive method of study, the reader is referred to the writer's book *Independent Bible Study*.

This study guide has been divided into eleven lessons in addition to a general introduction. The reader can choose for himself how many psalms of each lesson he wants to study at one time. Thoroughness, not speed, should be the determining factor.

The seven study aids that are given in this manual for the individual psalms are:

1. *Title.* The titles given are designated to indicate the main contents or character of the psalm. You should try to arrive at a title of your own as well.

2. *Occasion.* This is the historical incident or personal experience that gave birth to the psalm. Such information is not always available, nor always clear.

3. *Stanza divisions.* Analysis of a psalm depends on knowing where each new stanza begins. You will find this help invaluable in your study.

4. *Analysis.* The main purpose of this section is to present questions that will help you *search* and *dig* in the psalm. Most of the questions are so worded as to make you observe for yourself.

5. *Outline.* You may want to refer to the outline only after you have completed your independent study.

6. *Comments.* This brief section calls attention to certain aspects of the psalm.

7. *A practical lesson.* This is only one suggested lesson. You will derive many more from each psalm.

Many excellent commentaries are available if you wish to refer to outside help to supplement your own study. Among them are: W. Graham Scroggie, *The Psalms* (Westwood, N.J.: Fleming H. Revell Co., 1965); C. H. Spurgeon, *The Treasury of David* (New York: Funk & Wagnalls Co., 1881); J. J. Stewart Perowne, *The Book of Psalms* (Grand Rapids: Zondervan Publishing House, 1966); A. F. Kirkpatrick, *The Book of Psalms* (Cambridge: University Press, 1951); A. C. Gaebelein, *The Book of Psalms* (New York: "Our Hope" Publications, 1939); Kyle M. Yates, Jr., "The Psalms," *The Wycliffe Bible Commentary* (Chicago: Moody Press, 1962).

Remember that aids and methods do not guarantee success in Bible study. As you begin studying Psalms, depend on the Holy Spirit for light and discernment, and seek the face of the Lord throughout all your study. This testimony of Grace Saxe shows how fruitful such a study can be:

I want to testify to the great blessing which has come to my own heart through the study of the Psalms. . . . It has been one of the richest spiritual feasts I have ever known. Each Psalm, as meditated upon, has blossomed like a rose, imparting its own particular fragrance and beauty and inspiration and instruction. Through the study of the Psalms, more than any other part of Scriptures, have I come into a practical realization of God's greatness, love, nearness and sufficiency for all human need.

Suggestions to class leaders:

This book may be used for individual Bible study or for group work. When several are studying together, the leader may profit by these suggestions:

1. Determine how many psalms of each unit you will want to study each time. The number will vary from lesson to lesson, depending on the length and content of the psalms.

2. Constantly emphasize the importance of carefully looking up all Scripture references given to each lesson. This should not be neglected. The best commentary on the Bible is the Bible itself.

3. Encourage the members of the class to do some thinking and studying for themselves. Devote much of the class hour to a discussion of the members' observation and questions.

4. Remind the students that Bible study does not end with seeing what the Bible says but rather with going on to application. The sequence is OBSERVATION—INTERPRETATION—APPLICATION. Have the members write out personal applications derived from every psalm studied.

The Book of Psalms

Our study of Psalms will be more fruitful if we are first introduced to them as a whole, learning something of their background and general contents, before we become intimately involved in a detailed study of each individual psalm. This proper order of study is illustrated in everyday life by the *formal introduction* of one person to another and the *intimate friendship* that develops thereafter.

I. BACKGROUND

The psalms were not written in heaven for angels. They were written by men for men and have their original setting in the warp and woof of human experience. But like all the other books of the Bible, Psalms is a *unique* product of man. Although we do not know the mysteries of the book's *method* of inspiration, we do know (1) its original *source*—God ("Every Scripture is God-breathed," 2 Tim. 3:16, *Amplified;* "Holy men of God spake as they were moved by the Holy Ghost," 2 Pet. 1:21); and (2) the *end product*—it is indefectible ("Scripture cannot be broken," John 10:35), and it is profitable for man ("All scripture is . . . profitable," 2 Tim. 3:16).

Here are some of the "human" aspects of this book:

A. Name

When the individual lyrics of David and the other authors were brought together as one anthology, possibly as early as 500 B.C., the Hebrew title given to the anthology was *Tehillim*, meaning "praise songs." The Greek Septuagint translators gave the title *Psalmoi*, meaning "songs in the accompaniment of a stringed instrument," and this was the Greek title used in the days of Jesus (read Acts 1:20). Thus our English title *Psalms* is really an ancient title, even in pronunciation.

B. Place in the Bible

In the Hebrew Scriptures the scroll of Psalms appeared at the beginnings of the third division, called "Writings." (The three divisions of the Hebrew Bible are Law, Prophets, and Writings; cf. Luke 24:44.) As such, this collection of sacred songs was the inspired prayer and praise book of the nation of Israel. In the fourfold grouping of books in our English Bibles (Law, History, Poetry and Ethics, Prophets), the book of Psalms is the second of the third division.

C. Authors

The book of Psalms is commonly spoken of as David's because he wrote the larger number of individual psalms (seventy-three are ascribed to him in their titles).[1] He was known as "the sweet psalmist of Israel" (2 Sam. 23:1) and had an extraordinary combination of talents. On one occasion he was referred to as being "cunning in playing, and a mighty valiant man, and a man of war, and prudent in matters, and a comely person, and the Lord is with him" (1 Sam. 16:18; cf. 2 Sam. 6:5, 15; 1 Chron. 16:4-5; 2 Chron. 7:6; 29:25; Amos 6:5).

Twenty-seven psalms are ascribed to authors other than David, thus: descendants of Korah, ten; Asaph, twelve; Solomon, two; Ethan, one; Heman, one; and Moses, one.

Fifty psalms are anonymous. However, there is reason to believe that some of these were written by David. For example, Psalm 2 is ascribed to David in Acts 4:25. And Psalm 1 seems to be by the same author. Also compare 1 Chronicles 16:7-22 with Psalm 105 and 1 Chronicles 16:23-36 with Psalm 96.

David also arranged the Temple service of song (1 Chron. 25), probably writing much of its music.

---

1. The following is a classification of the psalms by authorship as designated by
   the superscription:
   David: 3-9; 11-32; 34-41; 51-65; 68-70; 86; 101; 103; 108-10; 122; 124; 131;
   133; 138-45.
   Descendants of Korah: 42; 44-49; 84-85; 87
   Asaph: 50: 73-83
   Solomon: 72; 127
   Ethan: 89
   Heman: 88
   Moses: 90
   Anonymous: all others

D. Dates

On the basis of authorship and historical references of some of the psalms, we may conclude that most of the psalms were written over a period of about five hundred years, between 1000 and 500 B.C., as shown by the accompanying chart.

1400 B.C.	1000	971	931	722	500
MOSES	DAVID	SOLOMON	DIVIDED KINGDOM	EXILE	RESTORATION
(PS. 90) plus?				(PS. 137) plus?	(PS. 126) plus?

MOST OF THE PSALMS WERE WRITTEN HERE

E. Style

The style of Psalms is mainly that of lyric poetry, three characteristics of which are very prominent:

1. Thought Pattern. Hebrew poetry does not depend on rhyme or meter as such, but is built around a thought pattern. This allows the author much liberty in terms of the structure of a single line and accounts for the large variety in line lengths, from very short to very long.

2. Parallelism. Most of the psalms are built around the structure of parallelism. There are various types of parallelism, some of the major ones being:

a. Synonymous. The second line repeats the truth of the first line, in similar words. Example:

"The earth is the Lord's and the fulness thereof; the world, and they that dwell therein" (Ps. 24:1).

b. Antibetic. The thought of the first line is emphasized by a constrasting thought of the second. Example:

"For the Lord knoweth the way of the righteous: but the way of the ungodly shall perish" (Ps. 1:6).

c. Synthetic. The second line explains or adds something to the first. Example:

"The law of the Lord is perfect converting the soul" (Ps. 19:7*a*).

3. Subjective Testimony. Whatever is written is the personal experience, thoughts, and emotions of the author. In choosing words to give such a testimony, the Hebrew author avoids abstract philosophical and theological terms, and uses concrete and pictorial ones. It is helpful to keep this in mind for understanding the messages of Psalms.

II. SURVEY

A. Arrangement

From ancient times the one hundred fifty psalms have been divided into five divisions or books. We do not know the original reasons for the divisions, though apparently comparisons were made between each division and each book of the Pentateuch. The old rabbis are known to have called Psalms the "Pentateuch of David." The five divisions are shown in the accompanying chart.

	BOOK I 41 psalms 1	BOOK II 31 psalms 42	BOOK III 17 psalms 73	BOOK IV 17 psalms 90	BOOK V 44 psalms 107 150
DOXOLOGY AT ➡	41:13	72:18-19	89:52	106:48	150:6
WORSHIP THEME	ADORING WORSHIP	WONDERING WORSHIP	CEASELESS WORSHIP	SUBMISSIVE WORSHIP	PERFECTED WORSHIP
Topical Likenesses to Pentateuch	Genesis —man—	Exodus —Israel—	Leviticus —sanctuary—	Numbers —Moses and wilderness—	Deuteronomy —Law and land—
AUTHORS	MAINLY (or all) DAVID'S	MAINLY DAVID'S AND KORAH'S	MAINLY ASAPH'S	MAINLY ANONYMOUS	MAINLY DAVID'S
Possible stages of collection	Original group by David	Books II and III added during reigns of Hezekiah and Josiah		Miscellaneous collections compiled in times of Ezra and Nehemiah	

In your study of Psalms you may want to look further into the apparent similarities of the five books of Psalms to the five books of the Pentateuch, as to topical content.

Note that a doxology appears at the end of each book. G. Campbell Morgan sees the doxologies as the clue to the content of each of the five divisions. He says that an examination of the doxologies "will reveal a certain conception of God, and an attitude of the soul in worship resulting from such conception."[2] His outline centered on "worship" is shown in the accompanying chart.

2. G. Campbell Morgan, *Notes on the Psalms* (New York: Revell, 1947), p. 9.

10

B. Superscriptions

All but thirty-four of the psalms have superscriptions, sometimes referred to as titles. These were not part of the original psalms but were added later, probably at least before 200 B.C. In the superscriptions are words indicating such things as (1) occasion of the psalm; (2) type of psalm (e.g., *tepillah*, "prayer"); and (3) musical instructions (e.g., *lammenasseah*, "to the choir leader"). The superscriptions do not have the weight of dependability as does the inspired biblical text itself, but the best rule of thumb to follow is to accept them as they stand.

C. Types

Many subjects are treated by the psalms, therefore they have a wide application. The psalmist may be reviewing the past (history); envisioning the future (prophecy); or reflecting the present (experience). In all of the psalms the writer is responding to the fact of a living God and His relation to men. Thus it is not surprising to find that the outstanding subjects of the psalms have to do with God: the person of God, the Son of God, the Word of God, the works of God, and the people of God.

When classified more specifically as to subject matter and attitude of writing, many types emerge. These are the major types.

1. Didactic. (E.g., Pss. 1, 5, 7, 15, 17, 50, 73, 94, 101.) Such psalms might be called psalms of formal instruction.

2. History. (E.g., Pss. 78, 105, 106, 136.) These psalms are almost wholly composed of references to historical events of the nation of Israel. A summary of the highlights of practically all of Israel's history is given in the historical psalms. References to historical events appear frequently throughout the book of Psalms.

3. Hallelujah. (E.g., Pss. 106, 111-13, 115-17, 135, 146-50.) The theme of praise in these psalms is obvious.

4. Penitential (E.g., Pss. 6, 32, 38, 51, 102, 130, 143.) Confession of sin occupies the greater part of each of these. Psalm 51 is the classic example of this type of psalm.

5. Supplication. (E.g., Ps. 86.) The psalmist cries to God in his own need, or he intercedes for another's need.

6. Thanksgiving. (E.g., Pss. 16, 18.) The note of praise and thanksgiving pervades the whole book of Psalms, but some individual psalms are particularly thanksgiving psalms.

7. Messianic. Psalms prophesies of the suffering and sorrows of God's people Israel and their coming deliverance, restoration,

and blessing. It prophesies of the coming kingdom and its glories. But most of all it prophesies of Christ in His two advents: His first advent in humiliation, and His second advent in glory.

The chief prophecies about Christ are contained in what are known as the messianic psalms. In these psalms not only is Christ referred to, but He actually speaks. And in these psalms we get the most wonderful glimpses into the inner heart-life of Jesus. The following example will illustrate this. We read in the gospel story, Matthew 27:35-36, that men nailed Jesus to the cross; that they parted His garments among them and cast lots over His vesture; that they sat around the cross and watched His sufferings. But do we know what was passing through the mind and heart of our blessed Lord as He hung there bearing the penalty of sin for a lost world of men? The gospels give very little light on this. It is Psalm 22 that affords us the experience of listening to Jesus communing with His Father in that dread hour.

Notice that Matthew 27:35 states that Psalm 22 is a prophecy of Christ. We recognize the agonized cry of the first verse, and such verses as 16 and 18 of this psalm show that the prophecy goes far beyond any of David's experiences.

The messianic psalms speak of Christ as the royal Messiah (Pss. 2, 18, 20-21, 45, 61, 72, 89, 110, 132); the suffering Messiah (Pss. 22, 35, 41, 55, 69, 109); and the Son of Man (Pss. 16, 40). Other messianic psalms are: Psalms 23-24, 31, 50, 68, 96-98, 102, 118.

Psalms contains the most minute prophecies of Christ in all the Bible. If we wish to know the full meaning of Psalms we must recognize its prophetic outlook.

8. Nature. (E.g., Pss. 8, 19, 29, 33, 65, 104.) God's handiwork is an inspiring subject for any poetical writing.

9. Pilgrim. (E.g., Pss. 120-34). This group of psalms, each bearing the title Song of Degrees, was probably a hymnbook used by the Jews on their pilgrimage up to the Temple on the occasion of the national feasts.

10. Imprecatory. (E.g., Pss. 35, 52, 58-59, 69, 83, 109, 137, 140). The imprecatory (cursing) passages of these psalms are generally looked upon with a great deal of perplexity. Many cannot understand how such utterances could be acceptable to God. The problem is answered when one recognizes the age and the setting of their writing. Gleason L. Archer has written of this:

> It is important to realize that prior to the first advent of Christ, the only tangible way in which the truth of the Scripture could be demonstrated to human observers was by the pragmatic test of disaster befalling those who were in error and deliverance being granted to those who held to the truth. As long as the

wicked continued to triumph, their prosperity seemed to refute the holiness and sovereignty of the God of Israel. A Hebrew believer in the Old Testament age could only chafe in deep affliction of soul as long as such a state of affairs continued. Identifying himself completely with God's cause, he could only regard God's enemies as his own, and implore God to uphold His own honor and justify His own righteousness by inflicting a crushing destruction upon those who either in theory or in practice denied His sovereignty and His law."[3]

III. PRACTICAL APPROACH

Psalms is one of the most practical books in the whole Bible, wondrously suited to the human heart. It is especially dear to every child of God, perhaps because there is no experience of the believer that does not find its counterpart in the Psalms. Someone, in speaking of the whole Bible as "the Temple of Truth" and the different books as different rooms in that temple, has called Psalms the Music Room. Surely it is filled with heavenly music suited to man's every experience. Here the Holy Spirit sweeps every chord of human nature: from the low, wailing note of Psalm 51, to the high, exultant note of Psalm 24. That Psalms was a favorite book of the first-century believers is shown by the fact that of the New Testament's two hundred eighty-three direct quotations from the Old Testament, one hundred sixteen are from Psalms.

Two of the outstanding practical benefits of Psalms are described here:

First. It furnishes us with models of devotion. David, who wrote so many of the psalms, has given to a worldwide audience through the ages an insight into the rich and varied experiences of his life with God, to the extent that no other writer has done. Anyone familiar with David's life cannot fail to be struck with this fact. He was, at different times in his life, a humble shepherd boy, a servant in the king's palace, a successful warrior, a fugitive, a great king, an exile, an old man. He was sometimes poor and sometimes rich, sometimes hated and sometimes beloved, sometimes persecuted and sometimes honored, sometimes obscure and sometimes prominent, sometimes profligate and sometimes penitent, sometimes sad and sometimes joyful. But in all these varied experiences and under all these changing circumstances, David talked to God, pouring forth his heart, his thoughts, his feelings to

3. Gleason L. Archer, *A Survey of Old Testament Introduction* (Chicago: Moody, 1964), p. 437.

his Maker. David's utterances to God at these times are recorded in the psalms, and, as the psalms are inspired by the Holy Spirit, they show us what kind of talking to God and what kind of heart attitude is acceptable to Him when we too pass through similar experiences.

It must also be said that the psalms that were written by men other than David were also inspired in settings and soul experiences very much like those of David. In fact when one reads Psalms in one sitting it is very difficult to imagine that one man did not write them all! (Read, for example, Psalm 42, which is attributed to a son of Korah. Does not this sound like David?)

Psalms is a unique volume in the library of Scripture. In the other books there is more of *God speaking to man*, but in Psalms we mostly have *man speaking to God.* And man is here speaking to God under almost every possible condition and position, *and speaking acceptably*, thus showing us how *we* may speak acceptably to God under every condition and in every position of life. This is the crux of true and profitable devotional experience. The supreme example of one who used the psalms in His devotions was Jesus. (E.g., the "hymn" of Matt. 26:30, sung at the Last Supper, was probably a portion of the Hallel Psalms 113-18.)

Second. Psalms teaches truth in terms of human experience, not abstractly. Truth experienced is truth soundly learned.

There is a great difference between learning a truth with the *head* and learning it with the *heart.* There is a tendency for us to apprehend truth as a proposition, by the mind only, and then to just talk about it. David had learned the great truths about God and life especially by learning them experimentally. For example, David had learned the truth of the holiness of God through being brought to realize his own exceeding sinfulness and feeling God's abhorrence of it. David had learned the truth of God's love and mercy by being himself forgiven and restored to fellowship with his Lord. David had learned the truth of God's power to save from every foe by being himself saved from his enemies. David knew that God hears and answers prayer because his own prayers had been answered.

Oh, the blessedness of *experiencing* the truth of the doctrines we know! Psalms, being a rich repository of experimental knowledge, encourages the believer to seek that blessedness.

Suggestions for studying the psalms:

1. Study the psalms in their historical setting, when that can be determined. For some psalms, the superscriptions reveal the occasion of the psalm. For example, the superscription of Psalm 3

states that it is a psalm of David when he fled from Absalom, his son. By reading the historical account of this in 2 Samuel 15, the psalm becomes clearer. The section *Occasion* under each psalm of this study guide furnishes historical settings as far as can be determined.

2. Keep in mind the character of the psalm you are studying —whether it is a meditation, a prayer, a hymn of praise, a prophecy. This will help you to "feel" with the author as you study the subject from *his* vantage point and with his purposes.

3. Remember that the psalms are poetry. Notice the poetic devices used by the authors to say what they want to say. Some of the main ones are:

a. Simile: comparison of two things, usually employing the words "as" or "like" (e.g., "He shall be like a tree," Ps. 1:3).

b. Metaphor: comparison of two things without using the words "as" or "like" (e.g., "The Lord God is a sun and shield," Ps. 84:11).

c. Hyperbole: exaggeration for effect (e.g., "All the night make I my bed to swim; I water my couch with my tears," Ps. 6:6).

d. Personification: applying personality traits to inanimate objects (e.g., "All my bones shall say, Lord, who is like unto thee," Ps. 35:10).

e. Apostrophe: addressing inanimate things (e.g., "What ailed thee, O thou sea," Ps. 114:5).

f. Synecdoche: representing the whole by a part, or a part by the whole (e.g., "the *arrow* that flieth by day," Ps. 91:5).

4. Keep in mind the *law of double reference,* which applies to many of the psalms. For example, a psalm may refer immediately to David and the circumstances in which he found himself, but in its ultimate and full import the psalm may refer to Christ. Or, the primary prophetic reference of a psalm may be to a specific future event in Israel's history, whereas the ultimate reference may be an event in the end time, such as the coming of the kingdom.

5. Study each psalm with the determination to let it do something to your own soul. Meditate upon the truths and sentiments expressed. Let the Holy Spirit be your teacher. Put to practice what you learn.

IV. REVIEW

As a review of this introductory lesson, answer the following questions. See how much you have remembered without referring back to the pages of the lesson.

1. What is the meaning of the word "Psalm"?
2. Into how many "books" is the book of Psalms divided?

3. With what does each of these five books close?
4. Give the number of psalms in each book.
5. Why is Psalms usually spoken of as David's book?
6. How many psalms are directly ascribed to David?
7. Name five outstanding themes of Psalms.
8. Name the different types of psalms.
9. In your own words write a list of suggestions for studying Psalms.

Lesson 1
Psalms 1-10

Book 1, the first division of Psalms, contains forty-one psalms most —if not all—written by David. These psalms will be equally distributed over the next four study units. As mentioned in the introduction, you should study at any one time no more than what you can give ample concentration to. This may even be just one psalm at a time. The divisions of the study units are mainly to serve as organizational signposts of progress in your journey through the Land of the Psalms.

I. PSALM 1

A. Title

The Two Ways. The way of God and the way of man. The way of the godly and the way of the ungodly. The way of life and the way of death.

B. Occasion

This psalm was no doubt intentionally chosen to introduce the whole Psalter. In practically every psalm there is to be seen the godly and the ungodly, the superior advantages of the godly and their more glorious end. Compare this first psalm with the last of the psalms (Ps. 150). Compare also the first four words of Psalm 1 with the last four words of Psalm 150.

C. Stanza Divisions

In your analysis of this psalm, observe three stanzas, beginning at verses 1, 4, 6.

D. Analysis

The Analysis section of these studies should be the heart of your own personal study. Complete this original work before referring to outside helps (e.g., commentaries) or to comments that appear below.

Analysis involves two main processes: seeing and recording. For the latter, you record on paper what you see and what you conclude. It is suggested that you record your studies of each psalm on an analytical chart, as illustrated by the accompanying example.[1] Use the example as a model, and adapt your own type from it. You should record these items:

1. Identification of Stanza Divisions. The verse references are identified for each psalm. Note stanza divisions at verses 1, 4, and 6 for Psalm 1.
2. Key Words and Phrases of the Text. If the psalm is short (like Ps. 1) you may want to record the entire text. Record only the biblical text inside the rectangle.
3. Groups of Thoughts and Items. These and all other observations are identified outside the rectangle.
4. Emphasized Truths and Related Truths. Indicate these by underlinings, arrows, or other marks.
5. Outline Studies. Observe this example: His Life; What Regulates His Life; The Fruits of His Life.
6. A Title and Main Points Related to the Title. For example: *The Two Ways*: (1) The Way of the Righteous Man, (2) The Way of the Ungodly Man.
7. Spiritual Applications. Record these at the bottom of the work sheet.
8. Commentary Helps. After you have concluded your own study, you may want to record on your chart helps obtained from other sources. (Cite all sources.)

It will surprise you how much more you will see in the text once you begin to record your observations. Someone has correctly said, "The pencil is one of the best eyes." You will value having this permanent record of your study for future reference and for adding further studies.

Because of limited space in this manual, the Analysis sections of these studies will offer only a few questions and directions, which should be pursued in connection with your analysis. Let

1. Consult Irving L. Jensen, *Independent Bible Study* (Chicago: Moody, 1963) for a full description of the analytical chart method.

THE TWO WAYS

1
THE WAY OF THE RIGHTEOUS MAN

His life

What regulates his life

The fruits of his life

1

(BLESSED) is the man that

WALKETH NOT in the **counsel** of the **UNGODLY,**

NOR STANDETH in the **way** of **SINNERS,**

NOR SITTETH in the **seat** of the **SCORNFUL.**

but

HIS DELIGHT is in the **Law of the Lord**

and in **His Law** doth he

MEDITATE day and night

And he shall be like

A TREE PLANTED BY THE RIVERS OF WATER,

that **BRINGETH FORTH HIS FRUIT** IN HIS SEASON;

HIS LEAF also shall not wither;

AND WHATSOEVER HE DOETH SHALL PROSPER.

NEGATIVELY

POSITIVELY

CONSEQUENTLY

HE KNOWS THE LORD'S WAY

—defying the wind

2
THE WAY OF THE UNGODLY MAN

UNPROFITABLE —chaff

GUILTY —judgment

OUTCAST —congregation

4

THE UNGODLY ARE NOT SO:

BUT are like the

CHAFF which THE WIND DRIVETH AWAY.

Therefore

THE UNGODLY shall **NOT STAND** in the **Judgment,**

NOR SINNERS . . . in the **Congregation**

of the RIGHTEOUS

THE FIGURE

THE APPLICATION

—driven by the wind

SUMMARY

6

FOR **THE LORD KNOWETH** the

WAY OF THE RIGHTEOUS:

but the **WAY OF THE UNGODLY**

shall **PERISH.**

THE LORD KNOWS HIS WAY

them suggest other paths of investigation. Instructions concerning recording your observations on an analytical chart will not be repeated from lesson to lesson. Also, it will be assumed that for every psalm you will derive *spiritual applications,* which is the ultimate purpose of your study. These also should be recorded. Suggestions for analysis of Psalm 1:

   1. Look for all the contrasts of this psalm. For example, compare (1) the first word and the last word; (2) the tree and the chaff; (3) the consequences of the godly life and the ungodly life.

   2. Study the progressions: walketh—standeth—sitteth
   counsel—way—seat
   ungodly—sinners—scornful

   3. What three things are taught about the ungodly man by the terms "driveth away"; "judgment"; "congregation of the righteous"?

   4. What is meant by the word "knoweth" in verse 6?

E. Outline

1 THE GODLY MAN	4 THE UNGODLY MAN	6 SUMMARY

F. Comments

This opening psalm centers on man, with every line of the psalm making a reference to him and his ways. The last psalm centers on the Lord, with every line of that psalm calling for His praise.

The word "blessed" is a key word of Psalms. The first line of Psalm 1 accurately translated would read "Oh the blessednesses of the man that..." "This word 'blessedness' is not found in the singular in the Hebrew because there is no such thing as a single blessing; wherever there is one there is another."[2]

G. A Practical Lesson

There are only the two ways and the two ends. In which way have you decided to walk? Read Matthew 7:13-14; John 14:6; Proverbs 16:25. See accompanying chart.

2. W. Graham Scroggie, *The Psalms,* rev. ed. (Westwood, N.J.: Revell, 1965), 1: 48-49.

LIFE ⟶

DECISION DETERMINES DIRECTION

DIRECTION DETERMINES DESTINY

DEATH ⟶

II. PSALM 2

A. Title

God's King. As God chose David to be king and established his kingdom, so He has chosen David's great Son to be King of kings and will establish His kingdom (cf. Phil. 2:9-11).

B. Occasion

Psalm 1 introduces the whole book of Psalms; Psalm 2 may have been given its prominent position as the second psalm to introduce Book One of the Psalms. Psalm 1 speaks of the two ways of man, measured by relation to God's law; Psalm 2 speaks of the two ways, measured by relation to God's Son.

C. Stanza Divisions

At verses 1, 4, 7, 10

D. Analysis

What is the main point of each stanza? On the basis of the word "therefore" of verse 10, relate this last stanza to all that goes before. Study the contexts of the references to God's Anointed, God's King, and God's Son. On the phrase "Thou art my Son," read Mark 1:11; Matthew 3:17; Acts 13:33; Hebrews 1:5; 5:5; 7:28; 2 Peter 1:17. Observe these relations: earth setting (vv. 1-3) and heaven setting (vv. 4-6); nations (heathen) rage and Lord's wrath; the "Why" of verse 1 and the "Be wise" of verse 10.

E. Outline

This marvelous poem is in four stanzas of three verses each.

1 SIN ON EARTH	4 WRATH IN HEAVEN	7 SALVATION BY THE SON	10 INVITATION AND WARNING 12
words about the nations	words about God	words by the Son	words to the nations
Christ: The Anointed One	The Enthroned One	The Son of God	The Savior of Men

F. Comment

"Begotten" in verse 7 does not refer to Christ's *birth* but to His *resurrection*. See Acts 13:32-33.

In this psalm we are admitted to the counsel chamber of the wicked and to the throne of God.

G. A Practical Lesson

Those who will not bend must break (v. 9). Read Philippians 2:10-11.

III. PSALM 3

A. Title

God My Help

B. Occasion

David wrote this psalm over the experience of fleeing from his son Absalom. Read 2 Samuel 15–18.

C. Stanza Divisions

At verses 1, 3, 5, 7

D. Analysis

Study this psalm using this outline: "Many say" (first stanza); "But I testify" (remainder of the psalm). What kind of help is suggested by each of these (v. 3): "shield," "glory," "lifter up of mine head"? Apply to today. Notice the tenses of verses 5-7.

E. Outline

1	3 5	7 8
PLIGHT	PEACE	PRAYER

F. Comments

The word "selah" appears three times in this psalm (seventy-three times in Psalms). It is probably derived from the Hebrew root *salal* meaning "lift up." It was not to be read aloud by the reciter. Rather, it notified him "that at this point he should pause in his utterance and permit the music accompaniment to strike up; or else ... lift up his voice to a higher intensity or pitch."[3] The word "selah" often comes after an impressive statement, hence the pause for intensified reflection.

G. A Practical Lesson

Absalom had the crowds with him, but David had God. One with God is always a majority.

IV. PSALM 4

A. Title

God My Righteousness

B. Occasion

Probably the same as for Psalm 3

C. Stanza Divisions

At verses 1, 2, 6

D. Analysis

What do you learn about man from this psalm? About God? What are the bases for David's prayer in verse 1? What is involved in the phrase "set apart ... for himself" (v. 3). How is 6*b* the answer to 6*a*?

E. Outline

1	SUPPLICATION	2	COUNSEL	6	TRUST	8
—the enlightened life—		—the sanctified life—		—the enlarged life—		

3. Gleason L. Archer, *A Survey of Old Testament Introduction* (Chicago: Moody, 1964), p. 436.

F. Comments

David was "not trusting in his own righteousness, but God's righteousness (v. 1). The doctrine of imputed righteousness was apprehended by the spiritually enlightened in Old Testament, as well as in New Testament, times. For a further illustration of this in David compare the opening verses of Psalm 32 with Paul's application of them in Romans 4."[4]

G. A Practical Lesson

Joy, peace and safety are given to those who know God as their righteousness (vv. 7-8).

V. PSALM 5

A. Title

The Morning Watch (See v. 3.)

B. Occasion

Not stated. Any morning of David's life would have been a suitable occasion to call forth this song.

C. Stanza Divisions

At verses 1, 4, 7, 9, 11

D. Analysis

Observe the frequent use of synonymous parallelism (see p. 6) in each stanza of this psalm. Underline the synonymous terms in your Bible: stanza one—prayer terms; stanza two—sin terms; stanza three—divine attributes, and worship terms; stanza four—sin terms; stanza five—joy terms.

---

4. James M. Gray, *Christian Workers' Commentary* (Chicago: Bible Institute Colportage Assn., 1915), p. 217.

E. Outline

1 MORNING WATCH	4 UNRIGHTEOUS HAVE NO ACCESS TO GOD	7 RIGHTEOUS HAVE ACCESS TO GOD	9 EVIL TONGUES AND THEIR JUDGMENT	11 PRAISE TONGUES AND THEIR REWARDS 12

F. Comments

In the *American Standard Version* the words "look up" (v. 3) are rendered "keep watch." "In this Song the believer's life, within and without, is contrasted with the unbeliever's, both as to his talk (1-7), and his walk (8-12)."[5]

G. A Practical Lesson

Much depends upon how we start the day.

VI. PSALM 6

A. Title

Midnight and Dawn

B. Occasion

An acute trial through which David was passing which he recognized as God's chastisement for some sin (v. 1)

C. Stanza Divisions

At verses 1, 6, 8

D. Analysis

Note references in the psalm to the fact that David's trial was (1) physical, (2) spiritual, and (3) social. Analyze the first stanza especially concerning the supplication verbs (e.g., "rebuke me not"). Observe the attitude of penitence throughout the psalm.

5. Scroggie, p. 63.

E. Outline

1 THE PLEA	6 THE GRIEF	8 THE ANSWERED PRAYER 10

F. Comments

David dreaded God's anger (v. 1) and God's absence (v. 4).

G. A Practical Lesson

The midnight's trial becomes the dawn's deliverance, in answer to the prayer of the penitent heart.

VII. PSALM 7

A. Title

Song of the Slandered Saint (suggested by Spurgeon)

B. Occasion

The slanderous accusation of a man named Cush, during the days when David was fleeing Saul (e.g., cf. 1 Sam. 24:9-15)

C. Stanza Divisions

At verses 1, 6, 14, 17 (You may want to break this down into smaller stanzas.)

D. Analysis

What is suggested by the "ifs" of verses 3-4? What is the key note of stanza 6-13? Notice the repeated word that bears this out. Compare the beginning and end of this psalm.

E. Outline

1 ADMISSION OF HUMAN FALLIBILITY	6 APPEAL FOR DIVINE JUSTICE	14 ARRAIGNMENT OF THE WICKED	17 ADORATION BY THE PSALMIST

F. Comments

Read Matthew 5:11-12 for Jesus' comments about the persecution of slander that is experienced for His sake.

26

G. A Practical Lesson

Slander is hard to bear, but he who is wise will pray and sing praises to God.

VIII. PSALM 8

A. Title

The Glory of God and the Glory of Man

B. Occasion

Could it be that one night when David was out under the starry heavens, meditating on the vastness of the universe compared with man, the Holy Spirit put this matchless poem in his soul?

C. Stanza Divisions

At verses 1a, 1b, 2, 3, 9

D. Analysis

Identify a theme for this psalm from its "envelope" (i.e., the beginning and end of the psalm). The excellency of the Lord is seen in various things, including (1) the heavens (v. 1a), (2) babes (v. 2), and (3) man (vv. 3-8). How does the psalmist use these three illustrations to teach his point?

E. Outline

1a EXCELLENT NAME	ILLUSTRATED BY			9 EXCELLENT NAME
	1b heavens	2 babes	3 man	

F. Comments

"Man is the crowned king of creation, and under his feet all things have been put (6-8). . . . But the original purpose of God for man has not been fulfilled because of his sin; yet that divine design is not frustrated, for God Himself has become Man, and by the incarnation and sacrifice on Calvary, that is restored which by the first

Adam was lost.[6] Study these passages that quote this psalm: Matthew 21:15-16; Hebrews 2:6-9.

G. A Practical Lesson

The exclamation "What is man ...!" magnifies not man but God, who crowned him.

IX. PSALM 9

A. Title

A Triumphal Hymn

B. Occasion

David may have written this after one of his victories over the Philistines (cf. 1 Sam. 17).

C. Stanza Divisons

At verses 1, 3, 9, 15

D. Analysis

What is the dominant note of each stanza? Note the repetitions of "I will" (vv. 1-2) and "Thou hast" (vv. 4-6). At what places is praise specifically mentioned? Study the psalm using the accompanying outline.

E. Outline

[1] PRAISE	[3] THE LORD A JUDGE	[9] THE LORD A REFUGE	[15] THE LORD PREVAILS [20]

F. Comments

There is a prophetic element in this psalm, pointing to Christ's second coming to judge and to reign. Note verses 7-8, 17.

---

6. Scroggie, pp. 74-75.

G. A Practical Lesson

If we are in right relation to the Lord on the throne (vv. 4, 7) we enjoy the blessings of the Lord as our refuge (v. 9).

X. PSALM 10

A. Title

The Wicked Ruler

B. Occasion

Though anonymous, this psalm was no doubt written by David. In Psalm 9 he writes about external enemies (heathen nations); in this psalm he writes about internal enemies, specifically wicked men in places of authority in Israel who oppress the poor and humble (cf. vv. 2, 18).

C. Stanza Divisions

At verses 1, 2, 12

D. Analysis

Compare the opening of this psalm with the first verses of Psalm 9. Also compare the beginning and end of this psalm. What are the many descriptions given of the wicked man in verses 2-11? Whom is David addressing in verses 12-18? What is taught about God in these verses? Study the related thoughts of verses 1, 11 and 12. Contrast the phrases "the Lord is King" (v. 16) and "the man of the earth" (v. 18).

E. Outline

1 WHY?	2 THE WICKED	12 PLEAS FOR JUST RECOMPENSE 18

F. Comments

The word "poor" might be read as "meek" or "afflicted" (*Berkeley*). A.C. Gaebelein and James M. Gray have suggested that the "wicked" one of this psalm personifies the Antichrist at the end of this age, as described in 2 Thessalonians 2:3-9. The suggestion for this interpretation comes from the phrase "the man of the earth" (v. 18).

G. A Practical Lesson

Regardless of appearances, the Lord has not forgotten; the Lord sees everything (v. 11); the "Lord is King for ever and ever" (v. 16).

Lesson 2
Psalms 11-21

The psalms learned are the psalms practiced, and so it should be your constant purpose in these studies to relate the psalms to your own life. If one gets no spiritual food, guidance, or instruction from the study of the Bible, he misses the great purpose for which God gave the Book.

The eleven psalms of this study unit do not represent any designed section in the book of Psalms. Study these psalms as a continuation of Psalms 1–10. Do not study them hastily; give much time to meditation and reflection. And be sure to record your thoughts, including your own list of practical truths taught by the psalms.

I. PSALM 11

A. Title

Faith, No Flight

B. Occasion

David is reflecting here on the advice of friends to flee to some mountain for safety from his pursuer, who may have been Saul (cf. 1 Sam. 23:7-18) or his son Absalom.

C. Stanza Divisions

At verses 1, 4

D. Analysis

Compare the beginning of this psalm with that of Psalm 10. All of verses 1b-3 is the advice of David's friends. How sound was the advice? Analyze David's reply (vv. 4-7). Connect 3b ("What can the righteous do?") with 4a and 7a. How does 4a answer the statement of 3a ("If the foundations be destroyed")? David said, "In the Lord put I my trust" (1a). Did David know what kind of a person he was putting his trust in? What does this psalm reveal about who this Person was?

E. Outline

1	FLIGHT?	4	TRUST!	7

F. Comments

"Faith will do more for us than flight. Some people are very clever at retreat, and strong on resignation: but these may be but castles of the cowardly."[1]

G. A Practical Lesson

See Isaiah 26:3-4.

II. PSALM 12

A. Title

Evil Tongues and the Voice of God

B. Occasion

These were dark days of apostasy during the lifetime of David, when men were departing from the faith (v. 1) and when baseness was "given a high rating among the descendants of man" (v. 8, *Berkeley*).

C. Stanza Divisions

At verses 1, 5

1. W. Graham Scroggie, *The Psalms*, vol. 1, rev. ed. (Westwood, N.J.: Revell, 1965), p. 87.

D. Analysis

Compare the beginning and end of the psalm. Study carefully the first line, "The fool hath said in his heart, There is no God." How does the remainder of the stanza interpret this? Note the emphasis not on *words* but on *heart* and *deeds*. In verse 2 the Lord *looks*. In verse 4 the Lord *speaks*. What is said in verses 4-6 about the unrighteous? About the righteous? What great truths are taught by the concluding verse of this psalm?

E. Outline

1	CORRUPTION	4	CONFLICT	7	CONSOLATION
	none doeth good		workers of iniquity and people of God		salvation of Israel

F. Comments

Verse 1 defines and describes not *a* fool but *the* fool—the *preeminent* fool—whose corrupt ways show that as far as he is concerned God really does not exist. Such a one might be called a practical atheist. "There can be no good where there is no god."[3]

G. A Practical Lesson

A sinful heart bears sinful deeds, and the wages of sin is death.

V. PSALM 15

A. Title

The Guest of God

B. Occasion

This psalm, with Psalm 24, may have been inspired on the occasion of the moving of the Ark to Zion (2 Sam. 6:12-19). Or the psalm may have expressed David's deep thoughts when he was in exile and thus deprived of worshiping in God's house. At such a time he would be thinking of who were the *true* guests of God.

---

3. Scroggie, p. 100.

C. Stanza Divisions

At verses 1, 2, 5c

D. Analysis

Relate verse 1 ("tabernacle" and "holy hill") to 14:7a ("Zion"). What is the psalmist really asking in verse 1? How complete is the answer of verses 2-5? Observe what the psalmist says in the concluding line (v. 5c). How is this thought related to "abide" and "dwell" of verse 1?

E. Outline

1 QUESTION	2 ANSWER	5c SUMMARY

F. Comments

The upright man of this psalm is a complete contrast to the fool of Psalm 14, in heart, word, and deed.

G. A Practical Lesson

Fellowship with God (v. 1) and victory in the world (v. 5c) are the rewards of the righteous.

VI. PSALM 16

A. Title

Preservation for God's Children

B. Occasion

As he wrote the psalm, David was contemplating the all-sufficiency of the Lord and the satisfaction and fullness of joy that He alone gives. At least some of the psalm was written specifically about the coming Messiah (read Acts 2:25-28; 13:35), and so this psalm is classified as a messianic psalm.

C. Stanza Divisions

At verses 1, 7

D. Analysis

First study the entire psalm as expressing David's personal relationship to the Lord. Then study the second stanza as being the words of Jesus Himself. How is this passage used in Acts? Compare the first and second stanza, as to their main themes. Relate the first words of the psalm, "Preserve me, O God," to the last words of the previous psalm, "shall never be moved." Note: Read verses 2-3 thus: "O my soul, thou hast said unto the Lord, Thou art my Lord: I have no good beyond thee. As for the saints that are in the earth, They are the excellent in whom is all my delight."

E. Outline

1		7		11
	MY WORSHIP		MY JOY	

F. Comments

Because Christ, the holy One, arose from the dead, all His children have the glorious hope of resurrection. Read 1 Corinthians 15:1-4, 20-23. To be *preserved* by God (v. 1) is to be kept from the corruptions of the grave (v. 10). Beyond the grave? In the *presence* of God, with its unending *pleasures* (v. 11).

G. A Practical Lesson

If real joy is to be hand, only God can give it.

VII. PSALM 17

A. Title

A Prayer Hymn

B. Occasion

This was a typical prayer that David probably prayed often while being expressed by his enemies. The psalm is one of the five psalms with the title "A Prayer" (the others: 86, 90, 102, 142).

C. Stanza Divisions

At 1, 7, 13

D. Analysis

First stanza: What does David claim as a basis for being heard by God? What does David pray for in the second stanza? Study carefully the phrases of verse 15.

E. Outline

1 PLEA FOR A HEARING	7 PLEA FOR MERCY	13 PLEA FOR DELIVERANCE 15

F. Comment

Note the power of God's Word (v. 4). The Word enabled David to keep to the highway of God instead of walking in the paths of the destroyer. It will help us in the same way if we study and obey it.

G. A Practical Lesson

"The effectual fervent prayer of a righteous man availeth much" (James 5:16).

VIII. PSALM 18

A. Title

A Praise Hymn

B. Occasion

The superscription of the psalm identifies this. The background may be that of 2 Samuel 8. Read 2 Samuel 22 for a duplicate recording of this psalm.

C. Stanza Divisions

Major divisions at 1, 4, 20, 32, 46 (You may want to look for small breakdowns of each division.)

D. Analysis

Compare the first stanza (vv. 1-3) and the last (vv. 46-50). Each of the three stanzas in between stresses a main truth about the general subject of *deliverance by God*. Study the psalm carefully to discover the main thrust of each stanza. In your study you will find many wonderful lines that will have a special ring to them. Make a list of these when you are identifying the spiritual truths taught by the psalms.

E. Outline

1 DOXOLOGY	4 DIVINE DELIVERANCE ILLUSTRATED	20 BASES FOR DELIVERANCE	32 EXAMPLES OF DELIVERANCE	46 DOXOLOGY 50

F. Comments

"There is a sense . . . in which all through this psalm we may think of Jesus as referring to His own sorrows while on the earth. His deliverance from His enemies, and His triumphs over opposition."[4] For this the psalm is classified as messianic.[4]

G. A Practical Lesson

"I will call upon the Lord . . . so shall I be saved from my enemies" (v. 3). This is the only sure way of deliverance from any danger or trouble.

IX. PSALM 19

A. Title

Revelation of God

B. Occasion

David could have been looking into the beautiful skies of dawn when he was inspired to write this.

C. Stanza Divisions

At verses 1, 7 and 12

D. Analysis

Each stanza presents a different way by which God is revealed to man. Look for these. What attribute of God is prominent in each

---

4. James M. Gray, *Christian Workers' Commentary* (Chicago: Bible Institute Colportage Assn., 1915), pp. 173-74.

stanza? Study carefully the six lines of verses 7-9. Note that each line teaches three things. Organize your observations. Tarry long over this wonderful psalm.

E. Outline

1	GOD REVEALED IN NATURE	7	GOD REVEALED IN SCRIPTURES	12	GOD REVEALED IN EXPERIENCES	14
	—glory of God—		—holiness of God—		—grace of God—	

F. Comments

"This is one of the greatest Psalms, alike in its subject, profoundness, and comprehensiveness."[5]

G. A Practical Lesson

In the light of God's handiwork (vv. 1-6) and God's law (vv. 7-11), it remains a wonder that the Christian may call Him "my Redeemer" (v. 14).

X. PSALM 29

A. Title

God Save the King (The Septuagint translates v. 9 thus: "O Lord, save the King and answer us when we call.")

B. Occasion

The psalm was probably sung before the people, led by their king, went forth to battle. Psalm 21 is the hymn of praise sung *after* the battle.

C. Stanza Divisions

At verses 1, 6, 7

D. Analysis

Study the psalm with this in mind: The first and last stanzas are the words of the people, while the middle stanza contains the words

5. Scroggie, p. 123.

of the king (or high priest). What does the psalm teach about trust; kinds of help from God; insecure sources of help? Do you see anything of a messianic character about this psalm?

E. Outline

1 PRAYER FOR THE KING	6 TESTIMONY OF THE KING	7 ASSURANCE OF THE PEOPLE 9

F. Comments

The phrase "the king" of verse 9 may refer to God, not to Israel's king. Compare this line with verse 1a.

G. A Practical Lesson

Let us not wait until we are in the thick of the battle before we begin to pray.

XI. PSALM 21

God Saved the King

B. Occasion

Probably sung after victory in battle (a companion hymn to Psalm 20)

C. Stanza Divisions

At verses 1, 7, 13

D. Analysis

The first stanza is spoken to the Lord about the king. What is the Lord credited with doing and being in this stanza? The second stanza is spoken to the king. What is the theme here? Compare the accompanying outline with that of Psalm 20. How is verse 13 a fitting conclusion to both Psalms 20 and 21?

E. Outline

1 PRAYERS FOR THE KING ANSWERED	7 FUTURE VICTORIES OF THE KING ASSURED	13 PRAISE OF THE PEOPLE

41

F. Comments

Deep significance is to be found in the words of the psalm when we regard them as applied to Christ: verses 1-6 referring to His past victories and verses 7-12 to His victories in the future, at the end of this age.

G. A Practical Lesson

When God gives spiritual victories we should not neglect giving Him praise and publicly testifying to His goodness.

Lesson 3
Psalms 22-30

Pause from time to time while moving through the psalms to renew perspective and revive appreciation of their contemporary value.

Before beginning your studies of the next psalms, consider these questions:

1. In what different kinds of circumstances were the first twenty-one psalms inspired?

2. The needs and problems of people in Old Testament days appear over and over again in the psalms. Are they the same needs and problems of mankind today?

3. The theme of praise is repeated continuously. Can we praise God too much? How much should praise be found on our lips? Is praise by our actions acceptable as well?

I. PSALM 22

A. Title

The Calvary Hymn

B. Occasion

We know of no circumstance of David's life to which the psalm could refer. The psalm is messianic; in fact, its sole object may be prophetical. (Cf. 1 Pet. 1:10-11; Luke 24:25-26.)

C. Stanza Divisions

At verses 1, 19, 22, 27

D. Analysis

What is the theme of each stanza? Contrast the first half of the psalm (vv. 1-21) with the last half (vv. 22-32). What aspects of Christ's crucifixion are referred to in verses 1-21? Compare, for example, Matthew 27:33-46. Observe how the psalm moves from the silence of loneliness (vv. 19-21) to the praises of a fellowship (vv. 22ff). Think of Christ's death as having occurred between verses 21 and 22. In verse 22 He is the risen One with a great declaration. List truths about Christ's death and Christ's resurrection taught by this sublime psalm.

E. Outline

1 CRUCIFIXION OF CHRIST		22 RESURRECTION AND GLORY 31	
Suffering	19 Plea	Praise	27 Anticipation

F. Comments

We begin to grasp something of the spiritual agony of Christ on the cross when the force of the words "Why hast thou forsaken me?" hits us. The awfulness of such a forsaking, temporary as it was, is seen to be consistent only when one recognizes the awfulness of man's sin, which put Jesus on the cross.

G. A Practical Lesson

"No crown without a cross"

II. PSALM 23

A. Title

The Shepherd Psalm

B. Occasion

The shepherd scenes of this psalm were written by one whose earliest memories were those of tending sheep as a shepherd boy.

C. Stanza Divisions

At verses 1, 4, 6

D. Analysis

Study this grand psalm thoroughly, on your own, before reading any comments on it. Where does the name "Lord" appear? Who is addressed in the middle stanza? In your own words write what each line teaches. Are any scenes other than pastoral ones suggested by this psalm? How does verse 6 serve as a concluding verse? Note the time references of this verse.

E. Outline

1 GREEN PASTURES	4 DEATH VALLEY	6 HOUSE OF THE LORD

F. Comments

The all-sufficiency of Christ, the message of this "heavenly pastoral," is stated in this opening line of unsurpassed beauty, "The Lord is my shepherd; I shall not want."

G. A Practical Lesson

Am I a wayward sheep or am I *following* my Shepherd, loving Him, trusting Him, obeying Him?

III. PSALM 24

A. Title

The Crown Song

B. Occasion

Originally this psalm may have been sung when the Ark was moved from the house of Obed-Edom to Mount Zion (2 Sam. 6:12-17). In the Temple services this psalm was read every first day of the week (our Sunday).

C. Stanza Divisions

At verses 1, 7

D. Analysis

What is the tone of this psalm? Compare it with that of Psalm 22.

What is the main theme of each stanza? Compare the question of each stanza. What is the key phrase of the psalm? In what way does this psalm refer to a future day? Compare the main themes of the three psalms of the trilogy: 22, 23, 24.

E. Outline

1 WHO SHALL STAND IN HIS HOLY PLACE?	7 THE KING OF GLORY SHALL COME IN 10

F. Comments

COMPARISONS OF THE THREE PSALMS:

Psalm 22	Psalm 23	Psalm 24
1. The Calvary Hymn	The Shepherd Psalm	The Crown Song
2. The Cross	The Crook	The Crown
3. Dying	Living	Reigning
4. Saviour	Shepherd	Sovereign
5. Past	Present	Future
6. Grace	Guidance	Glory
7. **Good** Shepherd	**Great** Shepherd	**Chief** Shepherd
(John 10:11)	(Heb. 13:20)	(I Pet. 5:4)

G. A Practical Lesson

If we do not crown Him Lord of *all*, we do not crown Him *Lord* at all.

IV. PSALM 25

A. Title

David's Daily Prayer

B. Occasion

Probably written in the latter part of David's life (see v. 7)

C. Stanza Divisions

At verses 1, 8, 16

D. Analysis

What is the *general* content of each stanza? Study carefully the prayer requests of the first and third stanzas. Who are the ones whom God will teach and guide? (vv. 8-12). What does this psalm

46

teach about prayer? What is taught about God? How is the last verse different from all the others?

E. Outline

1 SUPPLICATION	8 CONTEMPLATION	16 SUPPLICATION	22

F. Comments

This is one of the acrostic[1] (alphabetical) psalms, so written to encourage its memorization and frequent recital.

G. A Practical Lesson

This psalm is a good example of how to pray to God in daily devotions.

V. PSALM 26

A. Title

David's Integrity

B. Occasion

Possibly when David had been unjustly accused of wrong-doing

C. Stanza Divisions

At verses 1, 4, 6, 9, 11

D. Analysis

What is David's prayer in the first stanza? In the last stanza? The high peak of the psalm is the middle stanza. Analyze it carefully. Compare the second and fourth stanzas: What is the common subject? How do the stanzas differ in purpose? On what basis could David make such strong claims of integrity? Observe the distribution in the psalm of the phrases "I have" and "I will."

---

1. Each verse begins with a different letter of the twenty-two-letter Hebrew alphabet.

E. Outline

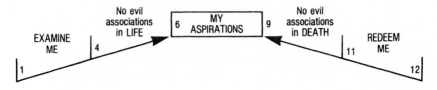

F. Comments

"Integrity" of verses 1 and 11 has at its root the idea of *truth*. This was an earmark of David's life, which made him a "man after God's own heart." Even in his sin he was quick to acknowledge the sinfulness of his heart. The reference in verse 9 to gathering is that of death.

G. A Practical Lesson

Only a truth-loving heart can render perfect praise.

VI. PSALM 27

A. Title

Confidence in God

B. Occasion

A time of trial, possibly warfare, in David's life

C. Stanza Divisions

At verses 1, 7, 14

D. Analysis

Compare the tones of the first two stanzas. Compare verses 1 and 14. How does verse 4 apply to the life of a Christian? Note the undelayed response of *8b*. Study the various prayer requests of verses 7-13.

E. Outline

1 CONFIDENCE	7 PRAYER	14 EXHORTATION

F. Comments

For a commentary on what it means to "wait on the Lord" (v. 14), study Isaiah 40:27-31.

G. A Practical Lesson

"If God be for us, who can be against us?" (Rom. 8:31; cf. Ps. 27:1).

VII. PSALM 28

A. Title

Prayer and Its Answer

B. Occasion

Some imminent peril of death for David

C. Stanza Divisions

At verses 1, 3, 6, 8

D. Analysis

Show how the psalm follows the accompanying outline. Observe where the psalm moves from "I" to "they." Note how this psalm, like many others, speaks much about David's enemies. When applying such verses to your own life, take the allowable liberty of seeing these as illustrations of *impersonal* enemies in your Christian experience, such as pride, unbelief, envy. Note how brief but all-inclusive are the four petitions of verse 9.

E. Outline

1 INVOCATION	3 SUPPLICATION	6 EXULTATION	8 INTERCESSION 9

F. Comments

When asked one day how he was feeling, a minister of the gospel replied, "I am weakness itself, but I am on the Rock." (See v. 1).

G. A Practical Lesson

We are to pray to the Lord for ourselves, but we must also pray for others.

VIII. PSALM 29

A. Title

The Thunderstorm

B. Occasion

Perhaps David was watching a sudden terrific storm that swept from the mountains of Lebanon in the north to the wilderness of Kadesh in the south.

C. Stanza Divisions

At verses 1, 3, 10

D. Analysis

Who is the main character of this psalm? Note how each line of the middle stanza describes some aspect of a thunderstorm. How are verses 1 and 2 an introduction to this description? Account for the presence of the phrase "beauty of holiness" (v. 2) in the context of a violent storm. How is the last stanza a fitting conclusion to the psalm? What important spiritual lesson is taught here? Of what in the Christian experience is the thunderstorm a figure?

E. Outline

1 CALL TO WORSHIP	3 THE STORM	10 THE CALM 11

F. Comments

The name "Lord" appears eighteen times in this psalm. Of His attributes, glory is the prominent one here. The inspiration for the original version of the grand hymn "How Great Thou Art" was the beauty of the Swedish meadows and lakes, viewed after a summer thunderstorm.

G. A Practical Lesson

"God is in the storm, not in nature's only, but also the soul's. He is in your storm. Do you believe that?"[2]

IX. PSALM 30

A. Title

Healing Psalm

B. Occasion

David's recovery from a serious illness. The connection between this psalm and the "dedication of the house of David" (superscription) is obscure. (Refer to commentaries for help on this.)

C. Stanza Divisions

At verses 1, 6, 11

D. Analysis

What different plights of David are cited in the first stanza? What is David's confession and prayer of the second stanza? How does the psalm conclude? Note the many antitheses of the psalm, for example, night and morning, mourning and dancing.

E. Outline

1 PRAISE	6 CONFESSION AND PRAYER	11 TESTIMONY 12

F. Comments

A paraphrase of 5b: "At nightfall Weeping comes as a guest to tarry; but in the morning Joy comes to stay."[3]

G. A Practical Lesson

David called only upon *saints* to sing God's praise (v. 4). Do we follow this example in our churches?

2. W. Graham Scroggie, *The Psalms,* rev. ed. (Westwood, N.J.: Revell, 1965), 1: 172.
3. Ibid., p. 176.

Lesson 4
Psalms 31-41

God himself is the key person of the psalms, for without him there could be no song at all. In studying the different psalms it is always interesting to observe how God is identified, whether by name, attribute, or action ascribed to Him.

Four names of God are prominent in Psalms: El, Adonai, Jehovah, and Shaddai. The meanings of the names, and the frequency of each in the five books of the Psalms, are tabulated in the accompanying chart.[1]

HEBREW NAME†	KING JAMES TRANSLATION	MEANING	BOOK I 1-41	BOOK II 42-72	BOOK III 73-89	BOOK IV 90-106	BOOK V 107-50
El	God	Almighty One	67	207	85	32	41
Adonai	Lord	Sovereign Lord	13	19	15	2	12
Jehovah	Lord	Covenant Maker and Fulfiller	277	31	43	101	226
Shaddai	Almighty	Provider; Blesser		1	1	1	

As you study the psalms of this unit, observe carefully the names of God[3] and the attributes that are ascribed to Him.

1. From W. Graham Scroggie, *The Psalms*, vol. 1, rev. ed. (Westwood, N.J.: Revell, 1965), p. 36.
2. Associated forms of the name words are included (e.g., Elohim is included under El). For an enlightening study on the names of God, see Nathan J. Stone, *Names of God in the Old Testament* (Chicago: Moody, 1944).
3. The King James text does not distinguish between Adonai ("Lord") and Jehovah ("Lord"). In the psalms of this lesson, the name Adonai appears at 35:17, 23; 37:13; 38:9, 15b, 22; 39:7; 40:17. (Use *Strong's Exhaustive Concordance* for identifying the names in the other psalms.)

I. PSALM 31

A. Title

My Rock and Fortress

B. Occasion

A time of trouble and grief (v. 9); weakness (v. 10); reproach (v. 11); loneliness (v. 12); slander, fear, and danger (v. 13).

C. Stanza Divisions

At verses 1, 9, 19, 23

D. Analysis

What is the main theme of each stanza? Study the context of each statement of trust. Note the various ways God is identified in the first stanza. Explain verse 22. Compare the first line and last line of the psalm.

E. Outline

1 CONFIDENCE IN GOD	9 APPEAL FOR HELP	19 ASSURANCE AND PRAISE	23 EXHORTATION 24

F. Comments

Some have identified the occasion of this psalm as being David's flight recorded in 1 Samuel 23. Because many parts of the psalm are striking parallels with Jeremiah's experiences, some think the prophet was the author.

G. A Practical Lesson

In any and all kinds of trouble God is our refuge.

II. PSALM 32

A. Title

The Pardoned Sinner

B. Occasion

Possibly David's sins against Bathsheba and Uriah. David's prayer for forgiveness (Ps. 51) may have been written first, followed by this psalm, wherein he testifies of the blessings of sins forgiven.

C. Stanza Divisions

At verses 1, 3, 8, 10

D. Analysis

Compare the introduction (vv. 1-2) and the conclusion (vv. 10-11). To whom is David speaking in verses 3-7? Who is the speaker of verses 8-9? Observe in the psalm the sequence: sin, repentance, confession, forgiveness. What is involved in forgiveness by God, and on what grounds can forgiveness be *justly* granted?

E. Outline

1 INTRODUCTION	3 PSALMIST TO THE LORD	8 LORD TO THE PSALMIST	10 CONCLUSION 11

F. Comments

This is one of the seven penitential psalms. David, as well as Paul, knew the truth of *imputed* righteousness. Compare verses 1, 2, and 5 with Romans 4:5-8.

G. A Practical Lesson

A pardoned sinner should praise (vv. 1-2); testify (vv. 3-5); instruct and exhort (vv. 6, 10-11).

III. PSALM 33

A. Title

Praise Becomes the Upright

B. Occasion

Apparently written to continue the thought of Psalm 32 and unfold additional reasons why the righteous should rejoice in the Lord and shout for joy. (Cf. Ps. 32:11 with 33:1).

C. Stanza Divisions

At verses 1, 4, 10, 20, 22

D. Analysis

How is the tone of the psalm introduced by the first stanza? Compare the second and third stanzas as to what is said about the Lord. What philosophy of history is taught by the third stanza? How does this psalm conclude?

E. Outline

1	4	10	20	22
CALL TO PRAISE	THE AUTHORITY OF THE LORD IN NATURE (Word)	THE SALVATION OF THE LORD IN HISTORY (Counsel)	CHORUS OF PRAISE	PRAYER

F. Comments

This psalm has much to say about two popular subjects of our day: (1) How did the universe come into being? and (2) What is the key to successful government?

G. A Practical Lesson

How marvelous to have such a God for our Father, as this psalm portrays.

IV. PSALM 34

A. Title

Thanksgiving for Deliverance

B. Occasion

Stated in the superscription and described in 1 Samuel 21:10–22:2. The name "Abimelech" may have been a dynastic name or royal title. (Compare the word "Pharaoh," used as both a name and a title for Egyptians rulers.)

C. Stanza Divisions

At verses 1, 11

55

D. Analysis

Notice the accompanying outline. In your analysis try to discover an outline within each stanza. What does the first stanza teach about praise? What does the second stanza teach about the *conditions* for reaping blessings?

E. Outline

1 THE SONG	11 THE SERMON 22

F. Comments

David was anxious that others should praise the Lord (v. 3), prove His goodness (vv. 8-9), and learn His way (v. 11).

G. A Practical Lesson

Blessing is conditional. Complete the following: If we _____ , He will deliver (v. 4); if we _____ , He will lighten (v. 5); if we _____ , He will save (v. 6); if we _____ , He will surround (v. 7).

V. PSALM 35

A. Title

Cry for Help

B. Occasion

Perhaps when David was being hunted by Saul (read 1 Sam. 24)[4]

C. Stanza Divisions

At verses 1, 11, 19

D. Analysis

On what common note does each of the three stanzas end? Relate this to the fact that this is an imprecatory psalm. What is the main

---

4. Some believe that David's words are aimed at Absalom's fellow conspirators. See J. J. Stewart Perowne, *The Book of Psalms* (Grand Rapids: Zondervan, 1966), 1: 301.

theme of each paragraph? Note the vivid picture of God as a warrior in verses 1-6. Observe the contrast between David's treatment of his enemies and their treatment of him (vv. 11-16). In what ways does this psalm describe the suffering Messiah?

E. Outline

1 DAVID'S DEFENDER	11 DAVID'S INNOCENCE	19 DAVID'S SCOFFERS 28

F. Comments

"The whole Psalm is the appeal to heaven of a bold heart and a clear conscience, irritated beyond measure by oppression and malice."[5]

G. A Practical Lesson

Injustice and ingratitude are hard to bear, but "take it to the Lord in prayer."

VI. PSALM 36

A. Title

Wicked Man and Righteous God

B. Occasion

Not known

C. Stanza Divisions

At verses 1, 5, 10

D. Analysis

Contrast the first and second stanzas. How does the last stanza fit into the psalm? How does verse 12 relate to verses 10-11? Make a list of the descriptions of the wicked man (vv. 1-4). What are the different descriptions of God in verses 5-9?

---

5. C. H. Spurgeon, *The Treasury of David* (New York: Funk & Wagnalls, 1881), 2: 155.

E. Outline

1 WICKED SINNER	5 RIGHTEOUS GOD	10 CONFIDENT SAINT 12

F. Comments

On verse 9: "There are some of the most wonderful words in the Old Testament .... They are, in fact, the kernel and the anticipation of much of the profoundest teaching of St. John."[6] (Cf. John 1:4, 9-10; 3:16, 36: 4:10, 14; 11:25-26; 14:6.)

G. A Practical Lesson

Every Christian life should be a striking contrast to the life of one who has "no fear of God before his eyes."

VII. PSALM 37

A. Title

God's Just Providence

B. Occasion

Written in David's old age (v. 25), after long years of experience and meditation. David wanted to answer the perplexing question of his day, "Why do the righteous suffer and the wicked prosper?"

C. Stanza Divisions

At verses 1, 12, 21, 32 (Note: This is an acrostic psalm, not easily divided into stanzas. Like the book of Proverbs, most of the verses are units by themselves.)

D. Analysis

Write a list of ten key lines or verses that teach great precepts. In your own words, what is the main theme of this psalm? Show how the psalm unfolds itself according to the accompanying outline.[7] Note references to future and final settlement of things (e.g., vv. 9-11, 34-37).

---

6. Perowne, p. 312.
7. Outline by Kyle M. Yates, Jr., in *The Wycliffe Bible Commentary*, ed. Charles F. Pfeiffer and Everett F. Harrison (Chicago: Moody, 1962), p. 509.

E. Outline

1 COUNSEL FOR THE WISE	12 DOOM FOR THE WICKED	21 REWARD FOR THE RIGHTEOUS	32 CONTRASTS OF RETRIBUTION 40

F. Comments

"Neither be thou envious against the workers of iniquity" (v. 1). Spurgeon comments, "Who envies the fat bullock the ribbons and garlands which decorate him as he is led to the shambles?"[8]

G. A Practical Lesson

Faith cures fretting.

VIII. PSALM 38

A. Title

Supplications of a Suffering Saint

B. Occasion

A time of chastisement for sin against God[9]

C. Stanza Divisions

At verses 1, 9, 15, 21

D. Analysis

Observe the references to the Lord at the beginning of each stanza. What is the main point of each stanza? In what ways was David suffering? What did he confess? What did he claim? What was his plea?

E. Outline

1 SUFFERING OF BODY AND MIND	9 SUFFERING OF PERSECUTION	15 SOURCE OF HELP	21 PRAYER 22

---

8. Spurgeon, p. 188
9. Some identify this sin as the adultery against Bathsheba, placing this psalm in this chronological series: Psalm 6, 38, 51, 32.

F. Comments

The opening of each stanza suggests an outline: (1) Rebuke me not, (2) You know me, (3) You hear me, (4) Forsake me not.

G. A Practical Lesson

David was perfectly silent when he was reviled (vv. 12-14). So was our Lord (1 Pet. 2:21-23; Matt. 27:39-44). Are we? Or do we "answer back"?

IX. PSALM 39

A. Title

Spare Me

B. Occasion

Probably the same as the previous psalm. Here David is reflecting further on his suffering.

C. Stanza Divisions

At verses 1, 4, 7, 12

D. Analysis

What was David suppressing (first stanza)? Relate this to the previous psalm. Observe that each of the next stanzas opens with a direct address to "Lord" (the second "Lord" is Adonai; the other two are Jehovah). What is the main point of each stanza? Verse 9 cites what reason for David's silence? Note that David asks God not to be speechless to him (v. 12).

E. Outline

1 ACCEPTANCE	4 HUMILITY	7 HOPE	12 PLEA 13

F. Comments

David compelled himself to refrain from murmuring and complaining before his enemies, but before God he poured out all his musings on the brevity, frailty, and vanity of human life. David was not a stranger *to* God, but a guest *with* Him ("for I am a passing guest with Thee, a transient, as were all my fathers," v. 12*b*, *Berkeley*).

G. A Practical Lesson

When despondent speak to God first.

X. PSALM 40

A. Title

Burnt-Offering Psalm

B. Occasion

Not stated (Compare Psalm 70 with 40:13-17.)

C. Stanza Divisions

At verses 1, 6, 11

D. Analysis

What is the tone of each stanza? What is the main theme of each? Compare the first line of the psalm with the last. Complete the accompanying outline, showing how each stanza may be broken into two parts. Study verses 6-8 in connection with Isaiah 1:10-15 and Hebrews 10:1-13. What lessons about witnessing can be learned from verses 9-10?

E. Outline

1 THANKSGIVING		6 CONSECRATION		11 SUPPLICATION	17
	4		9		16

F. Comments

This is a psalm of varied experiences. The circumstances of 1 Samuel 30 may have been the subjects of the psalm.

G. A Practical Lesson

"Thy law ... within my heart" (v. 8) is the right relationship of God's Word to the Christian.

XI. PSALM 41

A. Title

The Blessed Man

B. Occasion

Some time of serious illness (vv. 3, 8), and when David's opponent included even his "own familiar friend" (v. 9). For the latter, compare 2 Samuel 15:12; 16:20–17:4.

C. Stanza Divisions

At verses 1, 4, 10 (Note: Verse 13 should be considered separate from this psalm, serving as a concluding doxology to Book I.)

D. Analysis

How is this psalm similar to previous ones? Who is the subject of each stanza, and what is said about him in each stanza? What does this psalm teach about sin, mercy, and blessing? How does the psalm serve as a concluding psalm of Book I?

E. Outline

1 THE BLESSED ONE	4 THE HATED ONE	10 THE NEEDY ONE	13 DOXOLOGY FOR BOOK I

F. Comments

"Poor" of verse 1 refers to weak or afflicted ones. The doxology (v. 13) is especially significant when it is viewed as a concluding verse to Book I, because of all the varied experiences of the man of God described in the forty-one psalms.

G. A Concluding Exercise

Review your study of the first forty-one psalms, listing some of the prominent experiences of the believer that are the subjects of the psalms. Relate Psalm 41:13 to all of these.

Lesson 5
Psalms 42-55

This section begins Book II of the psalms, a group of songs which has been likened to the second part of the Pentateuch, Exodus, book of Israel's deliverance.

One of the prominent differences between Book I and Book II is the use of the divine name as shown as page 52. In Book I Jehovah (Lord) appears 277 times, Elohim (and associated words for "God") only 67 times; in Book II, Elohim appears 207 times, Jehovah only 31 times. In view of the meanings of these names (discussed in Lesson 4), what does this suggest? Another difference between the two books is that whereas most if not all of the psalms of Book I were written by David, many of Book II are attributed to various Levitical singers.

Before studying the psalms of this lesson, review the chart on page 10 showing comparisons of the five books of Psalms. Keep these things in mind as you proceed with your studies of Book II.

As you study each psalm of this lesson, make a note of a line or verse that proves to be of particular blessing in your own circumstances.

I. PSALMS 42 AND 43

A. Title

Thirsting for God (Note: Psalm 43 is a continuation of Psalm 42; the two may originally have been one psalm.)

B. Occasion

The writer[1] was heartsick because he could not worship in the Temple. Verse 6 suggests that he was located in the region of northern Palestine.

C. Stanza Divisions

At 42:1, 6; 43:1

D. Analysis

Note the similar ending of each stanza. Study all the questions of this psalm. Any questions directed to God? What is the tone of each stanza? What is the psalmist's problem or need? What is his heart hunger? What does the psalm teach about worship in God's house?

E. Comments

In 43:1 the psalmist appeals to God as his Judge, Advocate, and Deliverer.

F. A Practical Lesson

What is the deepest longing of your heart?

II. PSALM 44

A. Title

Perplexity

B. Occasion

A time of serious national distress (vv. 9-14), which was not the result of apostasy or idolatry (vv. 17-21) but rather was the test of loyalty to God (vv. 20-22).

---

1. The writer was probably a son of Korah. The King James inscription "for the sons of Korah" (in this and other psalms) should read "of (or by) the sons of Korah." Korahites were keepers of the gates of the sanctuary (1 Chron. 9:19).

C. Stanza Divisions

At verses 1, 9, 17, 23

D. Analysis

What era of Israel's history do verses 1-3 describe? What is the time element of verses 4-8? How does the second stanza (vv. 9-16) begin? What is the main theme of this stanza? How does verse 17 identify the theme of the third stanza? What is the spirit of the questions of the last stanza? How does the psalm end? Compare this with the first verse.

E. Outline

1 ISRAEL DELIVERED	9 ISRAEL ABANDONED	17 PLEA OF INNOCENCE	23 PLEA FOR HELP 26

F. Comments

This is a cry of people who were suffering for righteousness' sake as did Joseph, Daniel, Jeremiah, Stephen, the apostles, and many other saints. How important is religious instruction of children by their Christian fathers? (v. 1). Read Deuteronomy 6:6-7 and Ephesians 6:4.

G. A Practical Lesson

When perplexed by adversity let us stay ourselves on the blessed truth of Romans 8:28, 35-39.

III. PSALM 45

A. Title

Marriage of the King

B. Occasion

Probably the marriage of Solomon with the daughter of the king of Egypt (1 Kings 3:1). The psalm was inspired by the Holy Spirit with a prophetic purpose, showing Christ the King and His bride, the church.

C. Stanza Divisions

At verses 1, 2, 10, 16

D. Analysis

Study the psalm in light of its messianic purpose. From the description of the groom (vv. 2-9), what is taught here about Christ? Read the reference of Hebrews 1:8-9 to Psalm 45:6. What hymn of the church was inspired by verse 8*b* of this psalm? From the description of the bride (vv. 10-17), what is taught about the church? The main word of this psalm is "king." How does this help reveal the main theme of the psalm?

E. Outline

1 INTRODUCTION	2 THE KING	10 THE KING'S BRIDE	16 THE KING'S EVERLASTING FAME 17

F. Comments

"If verse 6*a* refers to a human king, it might be translated, *Thy throne is like God's.*"[2]

G. Practical Lesson

Jesus, who is our great King, our royal Lord, and our heavenly Bridegroom, deserves praise forever and ever.

IV. PSALM 46

A. Title

A Mighty Fortress[2]

B. Occasion

Perhaps such a deliverance as is recorded in 2 Kings 19:8-19, 35, in connection with Sennacherib's sudden abandonment of the

---

2. Charles F. Pfeiffer and Everett F. Harrison, eds., *The Wycliffe Bible Commentary* (Chicago: Moody, 1962), p. 512.
3. This psalm inspired the writing of Luther's hymn "A Mighty Fortress Is Our God."

siege of Jerusalem. Some have suggested the events of 2 Chronicles 20:1-30.

C. Stanza Divisions

At verses 1, 4, 8 (note where "selah" appears)

D. Analysis

Who is the central subject of the psalm? What main thing is said about him in each stanza? Note the occurences of the phrase "our refuge." Study the contrast given in verse 6. Who is speaking in verse 10?

E. Outline

¹ GOD AS HELPER	⁴ GOD IN THE MIDST	⁸ GOD THE EXALTED ONE ¹¹

F. Comments

Psalms 46–48 form a trilogy of praise, and all three may have been written in connection with some common deliverance.

G. A Practical Lesson

Compare this psalm with Romans 8:31-39, and list some truths the two passages teach.

V. PSALM 47

A. Title

King of All (cf. vv. 2, 7)

B. Occasion

Probably the same as for Psalm 46

C. Stanza Divisions

At verses 1, 5, 8

D. Analysis

How does this psalm expand on the truth of 46:10? Study the references to (1) *all* people, (2) nations (which are non-Jew and therefore Gentile), and (3) the chosen people of Israel. Relate Philippians 2:9-11 to this psalm. In your own words, what is the theme of this psalm?

E. Outline

1 REIGN PROPHESIED	5 REIGN CELEBRATED	8 REIGN INAUGURATED 9

F. Comments

"The three threads of Old Testament Prophecy, *Messiah, Israel* and the *Gentiles*, are all here. Messiah is to be 'the King of all the earth' (v. 7); *all nations* are to be His subjects (vv. 8-9a); and *Israel* has been chosen as the medium of accomplishments."[4] Spurgeon makes this comment, "The prospect of the universal reign of the Prince of Peace is enough to make the tongue of the dumb sing; what will the reality be?"[5]

G. A Practical Lesson

Is Christ King over all your living? King over your thoughts, deeds, and words? "That in all things He might have the preeminence" (Col. 1:17-18).

VI. PSALM 48

A. Title

City of the King[6]

B. Occasion

Probably the same as for Psalm 46

---

4. W. Graham Scroggie, *The Psalms*, rev. ed. (Westwood, N.J.: Revell, 1965), 1: 268.
5. C. H. Spurgeon, *The Treasury of David* (New York: Funk & Wagnalls, 1881), 2: 393.
6. Cf. Matt. 5:35; 1 Kings 11:13.

C. Stanza Divisions

At verses 1, 9

D. Analysis

What is the main subject of the first stanza? What attributes and works of God are cited in this stanza? Who is the central person of the second stanza? What descriptions are given of him here? How significant a conclusion is the last verse of this psalm? (Note the phrase *"this* God.")

E. Outline

1	THE CITY OF GOD	9	GOD OF THE CITY	14

F. Comments

God's presence in Jerusalem was her glory (vv. 1-2). God's presence in Jerusalem was her security (vv. 3-8). God's presence in Jerusalem was the reason for her worship, joy, praise, and testimony (vv. 9-14). It was in His Temple that God's people were led to meditate on His lovingkindness and righteousness (vv. 9-10). (Cf. Ps. 73:17.)

G. A Practical Lesson

If God dwells in your heart, His presence is (1) your glory, (2) your safety, and (3) the reason that you should worship, rejoice, and witness for Him.

VII. PSALM 49

A. Title

Limitations of Riches

B. Occasion

Perhaps the psalmist saw the godly poor around him, puzzled and discouraged because of the prosperity of the godless.

C. Stanza Divisions

At verses 1, 5, 14, 16

D. Analysis

Compare the question of verse 5 with the admonition of verse 16 (read 5*b* thus: "When the iniquity at my heels . . ."). What do riches fail to do or bring (vv. 5-13), 16-20)? What ultimate test is given riches in these stanzas? Are riches in themselves evil? Note that the third stanza (vv. 14-15) is set off from the rest of the psalm by *selah*. What contrast is made in these verses? How is verse 15 a key verse for this psalm?

E. Outline

1 SALUTATION	5 WHAT RICHES CANNOT DO	14 WHAT RIGHTEOUSNESS WILL BRING	16 ADMONITION 20

F. Comments

Death is no respecter of persons—rich and poor, wise and fool, high and low, all must die. In fact, in this sense man is "like the beasts that perish." Concerning money, it is not *money* but the *love* of money that is the root of the different kinds of evil (1 Tim. 6:10).

G. A Practical Lesson

A man's true prosperity is measured in light of the life hereafter.

VIII. PSALM 50

A. Title

Judgment

B. Occasion

A prophetic vision of the judgment was given to the psalmist and he wrote this dramatic and most impressive psalm to show the nature of true worship, to warn the wicked, and to encourage the pious.

*C. Stanza Divisions

At verses 1, 7, 16, 22

D. Analysis

Observe that the first stanza is a call to judgment. How impressive is the setting? Is this a judgment for all mankind or only for God's people? Study the next two paragraphs in light of your answer. How are "saints" identified in verse 5? What sins are alluded to in the second stanza? What does this stanza teach about true worship and about God? If "worship" is the area of life referred to in the second stanza, what area is the subject of the third stanza? What are the sins of the third paragraph?

E. Outline

1 CALL TO JUDGMENT	7 WORSHIP EXAMINED	16 WALK EXAMINED	22 CONCLUSION 23

F. Comments

The formalists were not censured for what they did (v. 8) but for *how* they did it. They had offered to God as though He had need (vv. 9-13), instead of making their offerings expressions of thanksgiving (v. 14) and in acknowledgment of their dependence upon Him (v. 15).

G. A Practical Lesson

Is our worship and our walk glorifying God?

IX. PSALM 51

A. Title

True Repentance

B. Occasion

When the divine message through Nathan made David see the greatness of his guilt, he wrote this, the greatest of the penitential psalms. Read 2 Samuel 12:1-13. (Note: This is the first of a new section of psalms [51–70] specifically ascribed to David.)

C. Stanza Divisions

At verses 1, 6, 13, 18

D. Analysis

What is taught here about sin, confession of sin, and the basis for God's forgiveness? (vv. 1-5). Study all the pleas of the second stanza. Be sure you understand what is involved in each one. Notice references to the spoken word in the third stanza. Let this be a clue as to what is the intent of this stanza. What is true praise? What is David requesting in the last stanza? Relate this to the entire psalm.

E. Outline

1 PRAYER FOR FORGIVENESS	6 PRAYER FOR RENEWAL	13 VOW OF CONSECRATION	18 INTERCESSION FOR ZION 19

F. Comments

David's actions were *wrongs* against Bathsheba, Uriah, and society, but they were *sins* only against God (v. 4). Sin is the transgression of God's law (1 John 3:4). David saw his utter defilement within and without, and understood that he could be cleansed only through blood and water (vv. 6-7; cf. Lev. 14:1-7).

G. A Practical Lesson

Purity as well as pardon is the desire of the true penitent.

X. PSALM 52

A. Title

The Evil-Speaking Man

B. Occasion

David's indignation at Doeg's betrayal of himself and Ahimelech. Read 1 Samuel 21:1-9; 22:1-18.

C. Stanza Divisions

At verses 1, 6, 8

D. Analysis

How do the first two words of the psalm introduce the subject of the psalm? Why was the line of 52*a* included in this context? What is the source of evil *words*? (See v. 3*a*). How thorough is the judgment of the boaster? What do verses 6-7 add to the appraisal of this man? Who writes whose epitaph? Contrast the last stanza with the first stanza. With what word does the psalm end? Compare this with the "mighty man" of the first verse.

E. Outline

1 BOASTER JUDGED	6 BOASTER LAUGHED AT	8 THE RIGHTEOUS PRAISE GOD 9

F. Comments

The boastful tyrant's power is short lived. The righteous man's trust is forever and ever (v. 8*b*).

G. A Practical Lesson

There is only one destiny of a deceitful tongue: to be rooted out of the land of the living.

XI. PSALM 53

This psalm is a revised version of Psalm 14. The writer makes some changes, chiefly in verses 5 and 6. Read both psalms together, noting the differences. Then read Psalm 53 again, following this stanza breakdown: 1-3; 4-5; 6. In what ways does the psalmist prophetically describe the religious conditions of the world in the last days?

XII. PSALM 54

A. Title

Assured Deliverance

B. Occasion

As stated in the superscription (Read 1 Samuel 23:19-29.)

C. Stanza Divisions

At verses 1, 4

D. Analysis

In stanza one, what is the psalmist's plight, and what is his prayer? What is meant by the phrases "by thy name" and "judge me," in verse 1? In the second stanza, observe the tenses of the verbs (e.g., is, shall, hath). Analyze this stanza keeping these tenses in mind. Some see in this psalm a prophecy of Christ, in particular a record of the passion of Jesus. Read it through with this thought in mind.

E. Outline

1 PLIGHT AND PRAYER	4 TESTIMONY AND VOW	7

F. Comments

God's "name" is His nature, the sum of His revealed attributes.

G. A Practical Lesson

A plea today for immediate help from God does not discredit yesterday's victorious experience or dilute our faith concerning tomorrow's situation.

XIII. PSALM 55

A. Title

Psalm of the Sore-Distressed

B. Occasion

Probably the time of Absalom's rebellion and Ahithophel's treachery, 2 Samuel 15–18.

C. Stanza Divisions

At verses 1, 9, 16

D. Analysis

What is the tone of each stanza? What is the main theme of each stanza? How desperate was David's grief (first stanza)? How do verses 11-14 and 21 identify a specific cause for David's grief? Write a list of spiritual truths about trust in God as is taught by the third stanza.

E. Outline

COMPLAINT OF PERSECUTION	9 DENUNCIATION OF THE WICKED	16 CONFIDENCE THROUGH PRAYER	23
—David's heart—	—Oppressor's lot—	—God's help—	

F. Comments

Note how repeatedly we are taught in Psalms that *trust* in God is the remedy for every kind of trouble. We may not complain *of* God but we may complain *to* God. Have not all of us sometimes felt David's desire to fly away from trouble (vv. 4-8)? To fly to God is better (v. 16).

G. A Practical Lesson

Write the truth of verse 22 indelibly on your heart.

Lesson 6
Psalms 56-72

The seventeen psalms of this unit compose the remainder of Book II of the psalms. All but the last two are ascribed to David.

One theme common to many of the psalms you are about to study is the persecution of the psalmist by his enemies. As shown earlier in this manual, this is another reason that Book II is likened to Exodus, for Exodus is the book of Israel's deliverance from the oppressor Egypt.

In applying these "enemy" psalms to your own Christian life, you may derive spiritual lessons for these circumstances:

1. Persecution from opponents of the gospel, because of your stand for Christ

2. Attacks from Satan himself, who "goeth about seeking whom he may devour" (1 Pet. 5:8)

3. Any hindrances in your life, such as sins or shortcomings.

The glorious truth of all the "enemy" psalms is that God is our great Deliverer, even as He saved Israel from the bondage of Pharaoh.

I. PSALM 56

A. Title

Fear and Faith

B. Occasion

Stated in the superscription (Read 1 Samuel 21:10-15.)

C. Stanza Divisions

At verses 1, 5, 12

77

D. Analysis

Note the punctuation of the *American Standard Version:* "I will not be afraid; what can flesh do unto me?" (v. *4b*); "I will not be afraid; what can man do unto me?" (v. *11b*). With this in mind compare the endings of the three stanzas. Note references to "daily" in the psalms. What place did David give to praise in his prayer life?

E. Outline

1 HELP ME	5 CAST DOWN MY ENEMIES	12 VOWS AND PRAISES 13

F. Comments

He who can deliver the soul from death can also deliver the feet from falling. "The machinery of prayer is not always visible, but it is most efficient."[1]

G. A Practical Lesson

Read verse 3 again.

II. PSALM 57

A. Title

Prayer and Praise Amid Perils

B. Occasion

When David "fled from Saul in the cave." Which cave? Adullam (1 Sam. 22) and a cave in the wilderness of Engedi (1 Sam. 24) are two possibilities.

C. Stanza Divisions

At verses 1, 7

1. C. H. Spurgeon, *The Treasury of David* (New York: Funk & Wagnalls, 1881), 3: 39.

D. Analysis

Observe that the last stanza, a hymn of praise, is repeated in Psalm 108:1-5. What verses in the first stanza speak mainly of God? Which speak mainly of the perils? Is there any pattern in the sequence? In what various ways are perils described? Count how many times God is referred to in these verses—by name and pronoun. Compare the phrases "calamities be overpast" (v. 1) and "heart is fixed" (v. 7). Compare this psalm with Psalm 56.

E. Outline

1 PERILS AND PRAYER	7 PRAISE 11

F. Comments

David's eyes and heart were constantly turned *upward*, on high, toward heaven, for his help (see vv. 2-3, 5, 10-11).

G. A Practical Lesson

In peril let it be true of us that our heart is fixed (not *fearful*, nor *fluttering*, but *fixed*)—steadfastly fixed on God.

III. PSALM 58

A. Title

Will Justice Triumph?

B. Occasion

A period during which those in authority were flagrantly unjust (Compare Psalm 82, which speaks of the same subject.)

C. Stanza Divisions

At verses 1, 6, 10

D. Analysis

How are actions (v. 1) related to the heart (v. 2)? Study carefully the descriptions of wicked men in the first stanza. In the second stanza, what one truth about judgment are the various figures of speech teaching? Compare "melt away," "pass away," and "take ... away." Whose is the "vengeance" of verse 10? What is the spirit of the righteous man's rejoicing in the concluding stanza?

E. Outline

| 1 | INJUSTICE ON A THRONE | 6 | INJUSTICE DETHRONED | 10 | THE SUPREME JUDGE | 11 |

F. Comments

The scales of acts and consequences will be seen in the last day to perfectly balance out. (Cf. Rev. 19:1-3.)

G. A Practical Lesson

Injustice on the throne of justice is a doomed situation.

IV. PSALM 59

A. Title

Surrounded but Saved

B. Occasion

As stated in the superscription. Read 1 Samuel 19:1, 10-12. Primarily David's own enemies are in view (vv. 1-2), but prophetically he sees the nations, in the last days, surrounding Jerusalem to destroy; and he voices the prayer and faith of the suffering remnant. "Heathen" in verses 5 and 8 should be translated "nations."

C. Stanza Divisions

At verses 1, 6, 11, 14

D. Analysis

Compare the first and third stanzas (e.g., "deliver me," v. 1, and "consume them," v. 13). Then compare the second and fourth stanzas (e.g., each stanza begins with reference to the enemy's "noise"; then appears the word "but"; this is followed by reference to a different sound). Observe how the second and fourth stanza end with recognizing the defense of God and the mercy of God.

E. Outline

1 PRAYER FOR DELIVERANCE	6 THE ENEMY AND GOD'S DERISION	11 PRAYER FOR JUDGMENT	14 THE ENEMY AND DAVID'S SONG 17

F. Comments

One justification for an imprecatory prayer is that in judgment the nations may "know that God ruleth in Jacob unto the ends of the earth" (v. 13).

G. A Practical Lesson

The song of the saint puts to shame the loud fury of the enemy.

V. PSALM 60

A. Title

From Scattering to Triumph

B. Occasion

Stated in the superscription. After a lost battle (vv. 1, 3, 10) and while contemplating another offensive (v. 9). Read 9*b* as "Who hath led me into Edom?" (ASV*). Read 2 Samuel 8:13-14 for background.

C. Stanza Divisions

At verses 1, 6, 9 (Note that 5-12 is repeated in Psalm 108:6-13.)

D. Analysis

What is the tone or atmosphere of each stanza? Show how the psalm proceeds according to the following sequence: sin, judgment, despondency, complaint, plea, promise, expectation, assurance, gratitude, and joy. What in verse 1 indicates that Israel had sinned? Study these phrases in the psalm: "Thou hast"; "I will." Note references to victory in the concluding line of each stanza.

*American Standard Version.

81

E. Outline

1	6	9	12
LAMENTATION	PROCLAMATION	EXPECTATION	

F. Comments

The holiness, sovereignty, and power of God are prominent in this psalm.

G. A Practical Lesson

It is a costly thing to displease God.

VI. PSALM 61

A. Title

An Exile Prays

B. Occasion

Perhaps during Absalom's rebellion when David was expelled from his throne (He was looking forward to going home again; see 2 Sam. 18.)

C. Stanza Divisions

At verses 1, 5

D. Analysis

What is the first actual petition made in the psalm? Identify the others. What are the picture words of verses 2-4 (e.g., rock)? What is the main point of verses 5-7? Observe the different words referring to "life." What is David's attitude in this psalm? How does the psalm end?

E. Outline

1	5	8
SHELTER	LIFE	

F. Comments

Exile is suggested by the hyperbole "From the end of the earth" (v. 2).

G. A Practical Lesson

Not only should we *sing praise* but we should *perform* our vows to God, verse 8.

VII. PSALM 62

A. Title

The Only Rock of Defense

B. Occasion

Probably the time of Absalom's rebellion (David is meditating upon all that God has meant to him throughout his life.)

C. Stanza Divisions

At verses 1, 5, 9

D. Analysis

What sins are cited in verses 3-4 and 9-10? What different aspects of "refuge" are taught by this psalm? Note the description of prayer in verse 8*b*; the truth about riches in 10*b*. How are verses 11-12 a fitting conclusion to this psalm?

E. Outline

¹ TRUST AND ADVERSITY	⁵ TRUST AND SECURITY	⁹ TRUST AND VANITY ¹²

F. Comments

"The confidence of the writer rises from stanza to stanza to a glorious climax."[2]

2. W. Graham Scroggie, *The Psalms,* rev. ed. (Westwood, N.J.: Revell, 1965), 2: 73.

G. A Practical Lesson

God is to be trusted "at *all* times" (v. 8), not only when the obstacles are small.

VIII. PSALM 63

A. Title

Longing of a Soul

B. Occasion

See superscription. Probably during the time of Absalom's rebellion. Read 2 Samuel 15:23-28.

C. Stanza Divisions

At verses 1, 5, 8

D. Analysis

Observe how each stanza opens with a reference to the soul. Let these references suggest the theme of each stanza. What is the time reference in verse 1: early in the day, or early in life? Compare verse 6. What is meant by "thy lovingkindness is better than life" (v. 3)? Note the places where praise appears in the psalm.

E. Outline

1 SOUL THIRST	5 SOUL SATISFACTION	8 SOUL TRUST 11

F. Comments

This psalm was adopted by the early church as the morning psalm (Psalm 141 being the evening psalm). Chrysostom said it was recited each morning as a "medicine," intended to "kindle in us a desire of God."

G. A Practical Lesson

God upholds those who follow hard after Him (v. 8).

IX. PSALM 64

A. Title

Consolation in Adversity

B. Occasion

A time when David's enemies were secretly plotting against him (vv. 2-4; cf. 1 Sam. 22; 2 Sam. 15–17).

C. Stanza Divisions

At verses 1, 7

D. Analysis

What does the psalmist say in the first two verses? In the last two? Compare verses 3-6 and 7-8. What does the psalm teach about the tongue and about retribution.?

E. Outline

1 WORKERS OF INIQUITY		7 CONSEQUENCES OF INIQUITY	10
God appealed to	3 Wicked men on the offensive	Wicked men fallen	9 God glorified

F. Comments

Note that the chief weapon that these enemies were using against David at this time was the tongue. Have you ever been the object of such an attack?

G. A Practical Lesson

> "Assail'd by scandal and the tongue of strife,
> His own answer was a blameless life."
>
> (Cowper)

X. PSALM 65

A. Title

How Great Thou Art!

B. Occasion

Perhaps a national thanksgiving festival at Jerusalem (The hymn of praise may have been composed for the festival, or inspired by it.)

C. Stanza Divisions

At verses 1, 5, 9

D. Analysis

Note the first and last words of the psalm. Compare this psalm with those preceding it that speak about the enemies of David. What is the tone of this psalm? Who is the central person? What is the main item of praise in each stanza? What does the psalm teach about God's grace and about His power? Study the subject of worship in each line of the first stanza. You will find this study rewarding.

E. Outline

1 THE GRACE OF GOD —in worship—	5 THE GREATNESS OF GOD —in the universe—	9 THE GOODNESS OF GOD 13 —in providence—

F. Comments

Nature itself paints a beautiful picture of praise. Note that even the pastures and valleys are filled with joy and song (v. 13).

G. A Practical Lesson

The more intimately we know God the greater our praise of Him will be.

XI. PSALM 66

A. Title

A Call to Praise

B. Occasion

Probably after some great national deliverance. (See vv. 8-12.) Some have suggested the deliverance from the Assyrian forces under Sennacherib (cf. Isa. 36–38). (Note that this and the next psalm are anonymous.)

C. Stanza Divisions

At verses 1, 5, 8, 13, 16

D. Analysis

Observe which lines are addressed to people and which are addressed to God. (Recall that all of Psalm 65 was spoken to God.) Note also where the psalm turns from plural pronouns to the singular pronoun. Make your own outline of this psalm, using the locations of Selah as further help. Another help is the clue of opening words, for example "Come and see" (v. 5) and "Come and hear" (v. 16).

E. Outline

1 UNIVERSAL PRAISE	5 NATIONAL PRAISE		13 INDIVIDUAL PRAISE 20	
Call to Praise	"See the Works of God"	8 "Bless God"	Consecration	16 Testimony

F. Comments

The prophecy "All the earth shall worship thee" (v. 4) does not refer to universal salvation but to universal acknowledgment of God as King of kings and Lord of lords (cf. Phil. 2:10-11).

G. A Practical Lesson

Many vows are made in times of trouble that are soon forgotten and never paid.

XII. PSALM 67

A. Title

"Thy Kingdom Come"

B. Occasion

The psalmist was thinking about Israel's mission to the world as

87

the messianic nation, the instrument for the establishment of God's universal kingdom. (Cf. Gen. 12:2-3.)

C. Stanza Divisions

At verses 1, 3, 5

D. Analysis

Note the identical verses 3 and 5. Identify the "us" of verses 1 and 7 and the "nations" and "ends of the earth" of verses 2 and 7. Why could this psalm be called a missionary psalm? How appropriate is the title "Thy Kingdom Come?" Compare this psalm (called by some "The Lord's Prayer of the Old Testament") with the Lord's Prayer (Matt. 6:9-13). How does the accompanying outline represent this psalm?

E. Outline

1 EVANGELIZATION	3 RULE	5 BLESSING 7

F. Comments

Some relate this psalm to Israel's Feast of Pentecost (harvest) or Feast of Tabernacles (ingathering).

G. A Practical Lesson

God reveals His way to the world through witnesses who reflect His glory (v. 2).

XII. PSALM 68

A. Title

The Triumphant Leader

B. Occasion

The psalm may have been sung when the Ark, the symbol of God's presence, was moving from the house of Obed-edom to Mount Zion (2 Sam. 6:12-15). It opens with the words of Moses when the Ark was beginning to move through the wilderness (cf. Num. 10:33-35).

C. Stanza Divisions

At verses 1, 7, 19, 32

D. Analysis

Beginning with the accompanying outline, analyze each stanza with the purpose of arriving at an outline within the stanza itself. What two groups are referred to in the first stanza? Notice how many times in this psalm God is mentioned. Locate the verses where He is pictured as the triumphant Leader. Study verse 18 in light of Ephesians 4:7ff.

E. Outline

1	7	19	32 35
GOD ARISETH	ISRAEL'S VICTORIOUS PAST	ISRAEL'S PROMISING PRESENT AND FUTURE	SING UNTO GOD

F. Comments

This psalm has been called "the grandest and most elaborate of all the Dedication Odes."[3]

G. A Practical Lesson

The Lord has given the Word. How faithful are we in publishing it (v. 11)?

XIV. PSALM 69

A. Title

The Sufferer

B. Occasion

The psalmist was suffering, though not for his sins. Prophetically some of this psalm refers to Christ, and in it we hear utterances of the Son of Man. For example, compare verse 21 with Matthew 27:34, 48; verse 9*a* with John 2:17; verse 9*b* with Romans 15:3.

3. Ibid., p. 102.

C. Stanza Divisions

At verses 1, 13, 22, 29

D. Analysis

What is the tone and main theme of each stanza? Compare the beginning and end of the psalm. According to the first stanza, how desperate was the psalmist's distress? In light of this, what is the significance of verses 13ff? Study these New Testament quotes of this psalm: verse 4, John 15:25; verses 9*a*, 9*b*, and 21 (see above); verses 22-23, Romans 11:9-10; verse 25, Acts 1:20.

E. Outline

¹ DISTRESS	¹³ DELIVERANCE	²² DENUNCIATION	²⁹ DEDICATION ³⁶

F. Comments

Let no believer think that he alone has suffered the uttermost until he has first read Psalm 69:1-12.

G. A Practical Lesson

Prayer in all circumstances should be the natural exercise of the Christian.

XV. PSALM 70

A. Title

Make Haste, O God

B. Occasion

Not known. The psalm is a repetition of the last five verses of Psalm 40, with a few variations. What stands out most prominently in these verses? Concerning the words "make haste" Scroggie has written, "The Father will quicken His pace when the child cries."[4]

---

4. Ibid., p. 120.

XVI. PSALM 71

A. Title

The Aged Saint

B. Occasion

When the psalmist[5] was old and in trouble

C. Stanza Divisions

At verses 1, 14

D. Analysis

Note the various time references in the psalm, especially those referring to the old age and maturity of the psalmist. Write a list of all the good qualities of this aged saint. What advantages balance any limitations?

E. Outline

1 MAINLY PETITION	14 MAINLY PRAISE 24

F. Comments

The psalmist did not hold back talking about the Lord (cf. vv. 15, 23, 24).

G. A Practical Lesson

As we grow older we should become stronger in prayer and praise.

XVIII. PSALM 72

A. Title

The Righteous King

---

5. The Greek Septuagint version ascribes the psalm to David.

B. Occasion

Composed by or for Solomon. But someone greater than Solomon is to be discerned here as "king," even the Messiah.

C. Stanza Divisions

At verses 1, 8, 15

D. Analysis

Make a list of the good attributes of the king of this psalm. Show how Christ fits many of these descriptions. Study the accompanying outline, and note how they represent the three stanzas. How appropriate is it for this psalm to appear at the end of Book II? How do verses 18-20 serve as a formal conclusion to this second book? Compare 41:13.

E. Outline

1 JUSTICE AND RIGHTEOUSNESS	8 SOVEREIGNTY AND GRACE	15 HONOR AND BLESSING 17

F. Comments

This psalm was used by the early church as the special psalm for the epiphany, "foretelling as it does the homage of the nations of the Messiah, of which the visit of the Wise Men was the earnest."[6]

G. A Practical Lesson

We are to wait for God's Son "from heaven, whom he raised from the dead, even Jesus, which delivered us from the wrath to come" (1 Thess. 1:10). Now read Psalm 72:17 again.

6. A. F. Kirkpatrick, *The Book of Psalms* (Cambridge: University Press, 1902), p. 418.

Lesson 7
Psalms 73-89

Of the seventeen psalms of Book III, only one is ascribed to David. The name Asaph is attached to the first eleven psalms of this group.[1] Actually, the identification of authorship is not crucial to a fruitful study of any psalm. Whoever the human authors were from psalm to psalm, each hymn has the unique quality of being inspired by the one Holy Spirit. There is thus a recognizable unity about the entire group of one hundred fifty psalms.

Many of the psalms of Book III speak about Mount Zion, its sanctuary, and worship by God's people. Thus the book is likened to the third book of the Pentateuch, Leviticus, where worship and the sanctuary are prominent subjects.

As you study the psalms of this unit, look for the things that give each psalm its distinctive character. For each psalm, record notations on the accompanying chart. Then at the end of the unit make a comparative study of the psalms on the basis of this tabulation.

I. PSALM 73

A. Title

Prosperity of the Wicked

B. Occasion

The perplexity of Asaph when he beheld the prosperity of the wicked (vv. 2-12) and the affliction of the righteous (vv. 13-14)

1. There may have been two Asaphs, centuries apart: one a musician of David and a seer (2 Chron. 29:30) who wrote Psalms 50, 73, 75-78, and 82; and another living during the days of the captivity, who may have written 74, 79, and 83.

PSALMS 73—89

Psalm	Tone	Main Problem or Need	Main Attributes and Works of God	Main Traits of the Psalmist	Main Lesson for Christian Living
73					
74					
75					
76					
77					
78					
79					
80					
81					
82					
83					
84					
85					
86					
87					
88					
89					

C. Stanza Divisions

At verses 1, 2, 13, 23

D. Analysis

After you have read the psalm once, identify the function of verse 1. Note the effects prosperity has upon the wicked (vv. 6, 8-9, 11-12). Describe the psalmist's struggle in verses 13-16. Where did he find the solution? (The phrase "their end" in v. 17 introduces vv. 18-20. Verses 21-22 continue the thought of v. 17.) Observe in the last stanza the triumphant tone of utter faith.

E. Outline

1 INTRODUCTION	2 INEQUITY OBSERVED	13 INEQUITY EXPLAINED	23 TRIUMPH OF FAITH 28

F. Comments

The psalmist envied the wicked when he saw their present prosperity (v. 3), but when he saw their future he changed his mind (vv. 17-19) and was ashamed of himself (vv. 21-22). Two psalms similar to this are 37 and 49.

G. A Practical Lesson

True worship in the house of God will bring light and understanding to the soul (v. 17).

II. PSALM 74

A. Title

O God, Why?

B. Occasion

The subject of the psalm is the desolation of Zion and the Temple, which took place in 586 B.C. with the siege by Nebuchadnezzar (read 2 Kings 25:1-17). If the psalm was written as a prophecy, Asaph the seer, who lived around 1000 B.C., wrote it. If the reference to the desolation was historical, someone living later than David's time was the author. (Note: The word *machil* in the superscription means "instruction.")

95

C. Stanza Divisions

At verses 1, 4, 10, 12, 18

D. Analysis

Note that the first, third, and fifth stanzas are appeals to God. Look for key words. What is the psalmist praying for? What are the themes of the other two stanzas? Analyze these stanzas carefully. On what does the psalmist base his hope? Amplify the accompanying outline.

E. Outline

¹ APPEAL	⁴ ENEMIES' DESECRATIONS	¹⁰ APPEAL	¹² GOD'S WORKS	¹⁸ APPEAL ²³

F. Comments

The psalmist is puzzled at God's inaction. Why does He not move against the wicked when He is so powerful? (vv. 10-17). The psalmist closes this most earnest supplication without a reference to praise or trust. But he still has hope, or he would not have used the word "remember" so often.

G. A Practical Lesson

God's cause cannot lose. His name, His covenant, and His power are at stake.

III. PSALM 75

A. Title

God Is Judge

B. Occasion

Not known

C. Stanza Divisions

At verses 1, 2, 4, 9

D. Analysis

What is the tone of each stanza? In what ways is God shown to be sovereign? What does the psalm teach about divine judgment? How does this psalm answer the questions of Psalm 74?

E. Outline

1 INVOCATION	2 RESPONSE	4 WARNING TO THE WICKED	9 EXALTATION OF THE RIGHTEOUS 10

F. Comments

"The Psalm is important out of all proportion to its length, for it is a revelation of the principle of God's government of the world, of His action in human history."[2] In times of anarchy and threatened dissolution of all things the Lord upholds and sustains (v. 3).

G. A Practical Lesson

God is sovereign over all nations. They rise and fall at His bidding. (Cf. Dan. 4:17, 32, 35.)

IV. PSALM 76

A. Title

Our Glorious God

B. Occasion

Possibly a victory over an enemy of Israel (Cf. 2 Kings 19:32-36.)

C. Stanza Divisions

At verses 1, 4, 7, 10

D. Analysis

What is the main point of each stanza? Study the accompanying outline; then observe how this brief outline on "Overthrow"

2. W. Graham Scroggie, *The Psalms,* rev. ed. (Westwood, N.J.: Revell, 1965), 2: 154.

represents this psalm: 1. Completeness of Overthrow (vv. 1-3); 2. Manner of Overflow (vv. 4-6); 3. Reason for Overthrow (vv. 7-9); 4. Result of Overthrow (vv. 10-12). Relate this psalm to Psalm 75.

E. Outline

1 NAME OF GOD	4 ACTS OF GOD	7 JUDGMENT OF GOD	10 WORSHIP OF GOD 12

F. Comments

This psalm is associated in theme with Psalms 46-48 and 75.

G. A Practical Lesson

Are we as quick to thank God for help as we are to seek that help? (Read again v. 11.)

V. PSALM 77

A. Title

Remember What God Hath Wrought

B. Occasion

A time of deep trouble (v. 2).

C. Stanza Divisions

At verses 1, 4, 10, 16

D. Analysis

Note how the first stanza introduces the entire psalm, by referring to the *problem*, the *prayer,* and the *answer.* Study the six questions of verses 7-9. According to the third stanza, what was the key to the psalmist's finding consolation for his soul? What do verses 16-20 add to this psalm? What do you think is the main teaching of this psalm?

E. Outline

1	THE DISTRESS		10	THE COMFORT	20
Introduction	4	Present distress described	The tonic of remembrance	16	Past deliverances described

F. Comments

The psalmist doubted God's tender mercies, and then realized that his doubt was his infirmity (v. 10).

G. A Practical Lesson

Meditation of God helps you; talking of God helps others (v. 12).

VI. PSALM 78

A. Title

A Parable of History (v. 2)

B. Occasion

Some have associated the recitation of this psalm to the removal of the sanctuary from Shiloh—in the land of the tribe of Ephraim—to Zion in the land owned by Judah, an event that implied the transfer of eminence from the former to the latter tribe. See verses 9, 41, 60, 67, and 68. Read also 1 Samuel 4:4, 10-22 and Jeremiah 7:1-3, 12-15.

C. Stanza Divisions

At verses 1, 12, 40, 54

D. Analysis

What is the main spiritual lesson of this psalm, as identified in the first stanza? What are the obligations and fruits of Bible instruction of children by their parents? (See vv. 4-8; cf. Deut. 6:6-7.) In the psalm note especially the various references to (1) the people's sins, (2) their judgments, (3) God's mercies. Read 1 Corinthians 10:1-12 for a similar treatment of the subject. Scan the psalm, and

observe who is the subject of most of the sentences. What may be
learned from this?

E. Outline

1 LEARNING FROM HISTORY	12 WILDERNESS JOURNEYS	40 DELIVERANCE FROM EGYPT	54 DWELLING IN- CANAAN 72

F. Comments

The historical record of this psalm is not given in a chronological
sequence, but logical. The third stanza (vv. 40-53) returns to the
signs referred to in verse 12 and describes them in detail.

G. A Practical Lesson

Where would you be today but for the mercy of God?

VII. PSALM 79

A. Title

Masterful Pleading

B. Occasion

Probably the Babylonian conquest, related in 2 Kings 25. If so, the
psalm must have been written by a later Asaph than the one of David's time, or it was written as a prophecy of this conquest. Compare also Psalm 74.

C. Stanza Divisions

At verses 1, 5, 10, 13

D. Analysis

Note how the psalm proceeds from lamentations (first stanza) to
praise (last stanza). How do the middle two stanzas account for
the change? Note the two parts of each of the two middle stanzas.
As you study the entire psalm, identify the grounds on which the
psalmist bases his plea for help.

E. Outline

1 LAMENTATION	5 WRATH AND MERCY	10 REVENGE AND PRESERVATION	13 PRAISE

F. Comments

The psalmist here is telling God that His glory and honor have been violated. It was God's inheritance the heathen had entered, God's Temple they had defiled, God's city they had destroyed, God's people they had slain and made a reproach, God's power they had challenged.

G. A Practical Lesson

God hears and answers prayers that seek His honor and glory.

VIII. PSALM 80

A. Title

"Restore Us"

B. Occasion

May have been the deportation of the northern tribes to Assyria (722 B.C.). The Septuagint adds to the superscription, "concerning the Assyrian."

C. Stanza Divisions

At verses 1, 4, 8, 14

D. Analysis

Observe the common refrain of verses 3, 7, and 19. "Turn us again" means "restore us." What are the psalmist's complaints in the second and third stanzas? Keeping these in mind, analyze the pleas of the first and last stanzas. Of what is the "vine" a figure in verses 8ff?

E. Outline

1 PLEA	4 COMPLAINT: "HOW LONG?"	8 COMPLAINT: "WHY?"	14 PLEA 19

F. Comments

Ancient Jewish scholars interpreted the "face" of verses 3, 7, and 19 to be the Messiah. In verse 17 "the man of thy right hand," "the son of man," is Israel, but typically it refers to Jesus the Messiah.

G. A Practical Lesson

When we are restored to intimate fellowship with God, then we behold His face in its shining splendor.

IV. PSALM 81

A. Title

What Might Have Been

B. Occasion

The celebration of one of Israel's feast days. Feast of Trumpets, Feast of Tabernacles, and Passover are suggested.

C. Stanza Divisions

At verses 1, 6, 8, 11, 13

D. Analysis

Observe that the psalm is divided into two main parts: summons to the festival (vv. 1-5) and the address by God (vv. 6-16). In verses 1-5 note the references to *hearty* praise. What does this teach? As you study each stanza of God's address, observe the progression of thought. How does the address end? Use this as a clue to the main intent of the psalm.

E. Outline

1 SUMMONS TO THE FESTIVAL	6 ADDRESS OF GOD			16
	Deliverance	8 Invitation	11 Rejection	13 Lament

F. Comments

"It is a sad thing when they who have been delivered from Egyptian bondage go into Babylonian captivity."[3]

G. A Practical Lesson

Sad, indeed, is the fate of those who refuse to hearken to God's voice until He gives them up (vv. 11-12; cf. Rom. 1:24, 26, 28).

X. PSALM 82

A. Title

Unjust Judges on Trial

B. Occasion

Probably the bribery, corruption, and injustice that Asaph saw around him.

C. Stanza Divisions

At verses 1, 2, 3, 5, 6, 8 (The stanzas are short, in keeping with the compactness of this dramatic and impressive psalm.)

D. Analysis

Study this psalm as a portrait of a court scene. Observe how verses 1 and 8 depict the setting. Follow the progress of each short stanza in regard to the main point given. What does the psalm teach about unjust judges?

E. Outline

1 THE ASSEMBLED COURT	2 THE TRIAL				8 THE GREAT JUDGE
	Indictment	3 Charge	5 Lament	6 Sentence	

F. Comments

The "gods" of verses 1 and 6 were the earthly judges of Israel, called "gods" because they were the official representatives of

3. Ibid., p. 189.

God's authority on earth. Read 2 Chronicles 19:6; Ecclesiastes 5:8; John 10:34-35.

G. Practical Lesson

We may count on God, the great Judge, to control this misgoverned world.

XI. PSALM 83

A. Title

Confederate Foes

B. Occasion

Not known, though many parts of the psalm point to the time of Jehoshaphat (cf. 2 Chron. 20:1-15)

C. Stanza Divisions

At verses 1, 9

D. Analysis

How is the opposition described in the first stanza? How thorough a judgment is asked for in the second stanza? What is the attitude and motive behind this imprecatory prayer? Study carefully the last three verses.

E. Outline

1 CONFEDERATE FOES	9 DIVINE JUDGMENTS 18

F. Comments

Enemies of God's people are enemies of God (vv. 2-3, 5; cf. Acts 9:1-5). What God *has* done God *can still* do (vv. 9-12).

G. A Practical Lesson

When spiritual foes combine to destroy us, let us commit all to God and trust him to overcome them.

XII. PSALM 84

A. Title

Heart Longings

B. Occasion

The psalm may have been written for the occasion of a pilgrimage to the Temple. David may be the author.

C. Stanza Divisions

At verses 1, 5, 9

D. Analysis

First read the companion psalm, Psalm 42 (also written "for the sons of Korah"), observing in the first two verses such words as "panteth" and "thirsteth." That psalm was written by one in exile, who could not go to the house of God. Now read Psalm 84, comparing its opening verses and keeping in mind that the psalmist has access to the Temple. Why is he so satisfied with the courts of God? Study each stanza in terms of the process of pilgrimage: Longing for God's House; Pilgrimage to God's House; Joy of Worship in God's House.[4] Note the contexts of the repeated phrases "Lord of hosts" and "blessed."

E. Outline

1 LONGINGS	5 PILGRIMAGE	9 WORSHIP 12

F. Comments

The Korahites were keepers of the gates of the sanctuary (cf. 1 Chron. 9:19). Verse 5b may be read, "In whose heart are the highways to Zion" (ASV).

G. A Practical Lesson

True subjects love the courts of their King.

4. Outline from *The Wycliffe Bible Commentary*, ed. Charles F. Pfeiffer and Everett F. Harrison (Chicago: Moody, 1962), p. 526.

XIII. PSALM 85

A. Title

A Patriot's Prayer

B. Occasion

Evidently a time of nation distress

C. Stanza Divisions

At verses 1, 4, 8

D. Analysis

First determine how each stanza differs from the others. Observe the different ways salvation is described in the first stanza. What is meant by "revive us again" (v. 6)? What do you learn about salvation in the last stanza? Study especially the word "righteousness." Explain "that glory may dwell in our land." What is meant by the two lines of verse 10?

E. Outline

1 ACKNOWLEDGMENT OF PAST ATONEMENT	4 PRAYER FOR PRESENT REVIVAL	8 PROSPECT OF FUTURE GLORY 13

F. Comments

Of verse 13, Scroggie writes, "That is a royal road to travel; see that its golden dust is on your feet."[5]

G. A Practical Lesson

Let us who love our country pray as did this patriot.

XIV. PSALM 86

A. Title

Hear Me, Lord (See superscription.)

5. Scroggie, p. 209.

B. Occasion

Not known

C. Stanza Divisions

At verses 1, 8, 14

D. Analysis

Underline in your Bible all the petition verbs (e.g., hear, preserve) in the psalm. Study these in connection with the *bases* of the prayers (e.g., *"for* I am poor and needy," v. 1; *"for* thou, Lord, art good," v. 5). You will learn much about prayer from this study. Notice how intensely personal this prayer is.

E. Outline

1 PRAYER OF A WEAK SOUL	8 PRAISE	14 PRAYER OF A PERSECUTED SOUL 17

F. Comments

"Observe the touching picture in verse 1, a child with his arms round his father's neck."[6]

G. A Practical Lesson

It takes an undivided heart (v. 11) to walk in the way of the Lord.

XV. PSALM 87

A. Title

Zion, City of God

B. Occasion

A meditation upon this favored city

---

6. James M. Gray, *Christian Workers' Commentary* (Chicago: Bible Institute Colportage Assn., 1915), p. 225.

C. Stanza Divisions

At verses 1, 4, 7

D. Analysis

Observe every reference to the city of Jerusalem in this psalm. What main point is established in verses 4-6? Relate this to the universal gospel. Who keeps records of who are the redeemed (v. 6)? Compare verses 1 and 7.

E. Outline

1 FOUNDATION OF ZION	4 CITIZENS OF ZION	7 FOUNTAIN OF ZION

F. Comments

In this psalm the kingdom age is prophetically in view, with Jerusalem as the center of the earth. Read Isaiah 2:1-4 and Zephaniah 3:14-17.

G. A Practical Lesson

Let us remember that people from all nations make up God's redeemed host.

XVI. PSALM 88

A. Title

Midnight Darkness

B. Occasion

May have been such afflictions as Job experienced. Some think the writer of this psalm was afflicted with leprosy. See verses 4, 5, 8, 15.

C. Stanza Divisions

At verses 1, 10, 13

D. Analysis

Observe the extremity of suffering in this psalm. Note the last word of the psalm. What is the point of the questions of verses 10-12? Note the familiar question, "Why?" The key inquiry you should make for this psalm is this: Was the psalmist counting on any kind of hope, and, if so, what was it?

E. Outline

1 LAMENTATIONS OF A SUFFERING SAINT	10 QUESTIONS ABOUT TERMINATED SERVICE	13 QUESTIONS ABOUT CAUSE OF AFFLICTION 18

F. Comments

This psalm has been called the saddest of all religious songs. The psalmist at least knew that the One to whom he was praying was the God of his salvation (v. 1). His help could come from no other source.

G. A Practical Lesson

Cling to God in the blackest of darkness.

XVII. PSALM 89

A. Title

The Covenant Psalm

B. Occasion

A season of great national humiliation—some think the Babylonian captivity. A time when God appeared to have forgotten His covenant (cf. vv. 3-4, 38-45).

C. Stanza Divisions

At verses 1, 5, 15, 19, 38, 46

D. Analysis

Note the many references to David and the covenant. Read 2 Samuel 7:18-16 for background. How do verses 1-4 introduce this psalm? What attributes of God are spoken of in the second stanza? How are the covenant people described in verses 15-18? What is the condition for covenant blessing? (vv. 19-32). Compare verse 39 with verse 34. What brought on the judgments? Note that the psalmist's question of verse 46 is not, "Why?" (cf. 88:14) but, "How long?" and, "Where?"

E. Outline

1 THEME STATED	5 GOD OF THE COVENANT	15 PEOPLE OF THE COVENANT	19 THE COVENANT	38 JUDGMENT OF THE COVENANT PEOPLE	46 SUPPLICATION 51

F. Comments

Verse 52, not a part of the psalm, sounds a note of praise at the end of this Book III similar to the doxologies we have already seen after Psalms 41 and 72.

A Concluding Exercise

Before moving on into Book IV of Psalms, review your study of Book III by completing the tabulation suggested at the beginning of this unit. Compare the different psalms on the basis of your tabulation.

Lesson 8
Psalms 90-106

Most of this unit's seventeen psalms are of anonymous authorship and constitute all of Book IV. From this point on in Psalms most of the hymns are of a liturgical nature, associated with public worship. In Book I they were generally personal, and in Books II and III generally national.[1]

Before studying each of the psalms individually, take a quick glance at the psalms to get a bird's eye view of where you will be traveling in this study unit. Look at titles and superscriptions in your Bible (if included in the edition you are using), and note the first and last lines of each psalm. This will give you a preliminary "feel" of the group.

I. PSALM 90

A. Title

A Prayer of Moses

B. Occasion

Written for the tribes of Israel during their wilderness journey between Egypt and Canaan. This is the oldest of all the psalms.

C. Stanza Divisions

At verses 1, 3, 13

---

1. See *The Wycliffe Bible Commentary*, ed. Charles F. Pfeiffer and Everett F. Harrison (Chicago: Moody, 1962), p. 528.

D. Analysis

What does Moses recognize about God in verses 1-2? What does it mean for God to be our "dwelling place?" (Cf. Deut. 33:27; John 15:4, 7; 17:24.) Study verses 3-12 for what they teach about time and man. What is the cause of man's frailty (vv. 7-8)? What is Moses' reaction (v. 12)? Study the prayer of the last stanza. What is the key to true rejoicing?

E. Outline

1 EVERLASTING GOD	3 TRANSITORY MAN	13 PRAYERS FOR BLESSING	17

F. Comments

This psalm is esteemed by many to be one of the loftiest of all human compositions.

G. A Practical Lesson

Let us learn how to value each day, so that we may "acquire discerning minds" (v. 12, *Berkeley*).

II. PSALM 91

A. Title

Absolute Security

B. Occasion

Probably similar to that of Psalm 90, since the two are companion psalms

C. Stanza Divisions

At verses 1, 3, 14

D. Analysis

Compare this psalm with Psalm 90. (E.g., compare 90:1 and 91:1; note the similar structure of stanzas; compare the outlines given in this study guide.) What does the psalmist say about God in verses 1-2? What man is being described in verses 3-13? Who is speaking in the last stanza? What are the promises? Compare "long life" (v. 16) with "soon cut off" of 90:10.

E. Outline

1 MIGHTY GOD	3 PROTECTED SAINT	14 PROMISES OF EXALTATION 16

F. Comments

The marvelous promises of this psalm are only for those who live in closest fellowship with God.

G. A Practical Lesson

This psalm has always been of particular blessing to Christians in times of war. Every Christian would do well to memorize the whole psalm.

III. PSALM 92

A. Title

The Sabbath Song

B. Occasion

The hymn was used in the Temple services for the weekly observance of the Sabbath.

C. Stanza Divisions

At verses 1, 6, 10

D. Analysis

What is the tone or atmosphere of each stanza? Observe references to God's "works" in verses 4-5. Meditate upon the works of God. Note the contrast: wicked man as grass (v. 7) and righteous man as cedar (v. 12). Be sure to list spiritual lessons taught by the psalm.

113

E. Outline

¹ PRAISE FOR GOD'S WORKS	⁶ THE WICKED PERISH	¹⁰ THE RIGHTEOUS FLOURISH ¹⁵

F. Comments

Much depends upon the soil in which a tree is planted.

G. A Practical Lesson

A righteous man can "still bring forth fruit in old age" (v. 14).

IV. PSALM 93.

A. Title

The Lord Is King

B. Occasion

The psalm was composed for use in the Temple services after the captivity. It may have been the prologue to an anthem of praise including Psalms 95-100 (read the first lines of these psalms again).

C. Stanza Divisions

At verses 1, 3, 5

D. Analysis

What attributes of God are recognized in each stanza? How do these enhance the Lord's kingship? What is intended by the statement that the world "cannot be moved" (v. 1)? What is symbolized by the word "floods"?

E. Outline

¹ MAJESTIC KING	³ MIGHTY KING	⁵ HOLY KING

F. Comments

"He is calm who believes that God is Sovereign."[2]

G. A Practical Lesson

The teachings ("testimonies") and character (e.g., "holiness") of God are unchangeable (v. 5).

V. PSALM 94

A. Title

God Will Do Right

B. Occasion

A time of oppression, possibly by foreign foes (cf. v. 5)

C. Stanza Divisions

At verses 1, 3, 12

D. Analysis

What does the psalmist recognize about God in the introduction? How do verses 8-11 answer verses 3-7? Why is blessing associated with chastening (v. 12)? What are the different blessings for the righteous man, listed in verses 12-23?

E. Outline

[1] THEME	[3] THE WICKED AND THEIR EXPOSURE	[12] THE RIGHTEOUS AND THEIR HELP [23]

F. Comments

Vengeance by God is not like a man's passion-fired revenge.

---

2. W. Graham Scroggie, *The Psalms*, rev. ed. (Westwood, N.J.: Revell, 1965), 2: 263.

G. A Practical Lesson

God has intimate knowledge of man's every act, word, and thought (vv. 8-11).

VI. PSALMS 95-100

This wonderful group of hymns about worship should lift the heart of any Christian. In these the psalmist's eyes are fixed on God, and hardly a mention is made of problems and troubles of the believer. As you read these psalms you will see what a good spiritual tonic they are.

For your analysis of these psalms, only a few guides will be given, appearing on the accompanying chart. Through the many kinds of questions posed in previous study units, you have received training in knowing what path of inquiry a Bible student should follow.

Review Psalm 93, which, as indicated earlier, may have introduced this group of hymns. Then study each psalm carefully, and record in condensed form your observations on the accompanying chart. Use the stanza divisions shown, to identify units within each psalm.

VII. PSALM 101

A. Title

Vows of a King

B. Occasion

The psalm was probably written by David early in his reign, when he wanted to resolve to God to be a good king.

C. Stanza Divisions

At verses 1, 5

D. Analysis

Observe how verse 1 is a response to the previous group of psalms. Note the different qualities of a good ruler recognized in verses 2-4. According to the last stanza what are marks of good government and society?

PSALMS 95—100

Psalm	Stanza Divisions	God	Worship	Main Exhortations and Warnings	Your Title for the Psalm
95	1-7 8-11				
96	1-6 7-9 10-13				
97	1-6 7-12				
98	1-3 4-6 7-9				
99	1-3 4-5 6-9				
100	1-3 4-5				

E. Outline

1	RIGHTEOUS RULER	5	RIGHTEOUS KINGDOM	8

F. Comments

This practical psalm is a good response to the psalms of worship preceding it, for true worship should produce righteous walk.

G. A Practical Lesson

"There cannot be a pure Court where there is a corrupt King."[3]

VIII. PSALM 102

A. Title

The Lonely Afflicted One

B. Occasion

Not known

C. Stanza Divisions

At verses 1, 12, 23

D. Analysis

Observe the extreme anguish described in the first stanza. How is the phrase "But thou, O Lord" (v. 12) a turning point in the psalm? Who is the main subject of verses 12-28? What attribute of God is emphasized in the second stanza? In the third stanza? Note how Hebrews 1:10-12 quotes verses 25-27. Interpret the last stanza in the light of this.

E. Outline

1	CRY IN SORE AFFLICTION	12	CONSOLATION OVER GOD'S MERCY	23	CONFIDENCE IN THE UNCHANGING GOD	28

3. Ibid., 3: 6.

F. Comments

In many ways this psalm speaks prophetically of Christ, as to His humiliation, exaltation, and glorification.

G. A Practical Lesson

It is a comfort to a Christian to know that God never changes.

IX. PSALM 103

A. Title

A Pinnacle of Praise

B. Occasion

When he wrote this psalm, David was truly soaring like an eagle.

C. Stanza Divisions

At verses 1, 8, 19

D. Analysis

Compare the beginning and ending of the psalm. How often does the phrase "Bless the Lord" appear? Who is mainly described in the first stanza? In the last stanza? What main attribute of God appears in verses 8-18? Does David ask for anything in this psalm?

E. Outline

1 THE LORD WHO IS PRAISED	8 THE MERCY OF THE LORD	19 THE SAINT WHO PRAISES 22

F. Comments

"This hymn of praise is without peer in all the world's literature. . . . The manner of expression and the depth of insight are remarkable for one living prior to the coming of Christ."[4]

---

4. *The Wycliffe Bible Commentary*, p. 533.

G. A Practical Lesson

Forget not all His benefits!

X. PSALMS 104

A. Title

God of Creation

B. Occasion

The psalmist meditates upon creation and the ordering of all nature. This psalm is a "poet's version" of the first two chapters of Genesis.

C. Stanza Divisions

At verses 1, 10, 24, 31

D. Analysis

What do verses 1-9 teach about God's sovereignty in His creative work? What reference to His providence appear in the second stanza? Observe the creatures' dependence on God in the third stanza. Analyze carefully the last stanza of praise.

E. Outline

1 DIVINE CREATION	10 DIVINE PROVIDENCE	24 CREATURES' DEPENDENCE	31 PSALMIST'S PRAISE 35

F. Comments

Verses 31-35 look forward to a new earth in which dwelleth righteousness.

G. A Practical Lesson

God is sovereign over history (Ps. 103) just as He is sovereign over nature (Ps. 104).

XI. PSALM 105

A. Title

God Delivers Israel

B. Occasion

A time of national thanksgiving for God's goodness. The first fifteen verses of this psalm were sung when the Ark was removed to Jerusalem (1 Chron. 16:1, 7-22).

C. Stanza Divisions

At verses 1, 7, 16, 26, 43

D. Analysis

Observe the various exhortations of the call to praise in the first stanza. Study the covenant of verses 7-15. Compare verses 42. Where in the psalm is verse 11 fulfilled? Observe how all the highlights of Israel's history are recorded in verses 16-42. What truth stands out prominently here? Analyze the brief triumphant conclusion. Why is obedience mentioned here?

E. Outline

1 CALL TO PRAISE	7 THE COVENANT	16 THE DELIVERANCES		43 THE INHERITANCE 45
		Haven in Egypt	Deliverance from Egypt	

F. Comments

This is the second of four classic songs of Israel's history, the others being 78, 106, 136. The practical design of all God's goodness to Israel was their obedience to Him (vv. 43-45). God desires the same obedience of His church today.

G. A Practical Lesson

"My God shall supply all your need" (Phil. 4:19).

XII. PSALM 106

A. Title

Israel Disobeys God

B. Occasion

The psalm was written as a confession of national sin. The psalmist reviews Israel's history from their deliverance from Egyptian bondage to their return from Babylonian captivity, a period of nine hundred years.

C. Stanza Divisions

At verses 1, 7, 13, 34, 47 (Verse 48 is a concluding doxology for all the psalms of Book IV.)

D. Analysis

Study the references in verses 7-46 to these subjects: sin, judgment, repentance, mercy, deliverance. What are your conclusions? In the light of these verses, analyze carefully the words of confession and plea in verses 1-6, 47.

E. Outline

1 CONFESSION AND PLEA	7 EXODUS EXPERIENCES	13 WILDERNESS EXPERIENCES	34 CANAAN EXPERIENCES	47 PRAYER

F. Comments

Whereas Psalm 105 relates how God treated Israel, Psalm 106 relates especially how Israel treated God. The latter psalm "begins and ends with Hallelujah—'Praise ye the Lord.' The space between these two ascriptions of praise is filled up with the mournful details of Israel's sin, and the extraordinary patience of God."[5]

---

5. C. H. Spurgeon, *The Treasury of David* (New York: Funk & Wagnalls, 1881), 5: 72.

G. A Practical Lesson

Our confession should be verse 6 and our prayer, verse 4.

Think back over the psalms of Book IV and write out a brief summary of their message. What have you learned from these psalms for your own spiritual edification?

Lesson 9
Psalms 107-119

Book V, which is the last group of the book of Psalms, begins with Psalm 107 of this lesson. Most of the psalms of Book V are written on the high note of praise. The opening psalm, Psalm 107, continually appeals to men to praise the Lord. The concluding group of psalms, 146-50, are the loudest outbursts of praise throughout the psalter.

If one is looking for a comparision of Book V with the fifth book of the pentateuch, Deuteronomy, the outstanding parallels are that both books are about the law and the land. Concerning the former, the classic Scripture on the subject of the Word of God is Psalm 119.

I. PSALM 107

A. Title

The Song of the Redeemed (v. 2)

B. Occasion

The psalm was suggested by God's providential deliverances of Israel, probably soon after returning from exile (see vv. 2-3).

C. Stanza Divisions

At verses 1, 4, 10, 17, 23, 33

D. Analysis

Observe the common refrain concluding stanza 2-5. What need is represented by each of these stanzas? Note the four cries. How does the Lord help in each need? What do verses 33-43 add to the psalm?

E. Outline

1 4	DELIVERANCES OF GOD				33 43
CALL TO PRAISE	FROM WANDERING	10 FROM BONDAGE	17 FROM SICKNESS	23 FROM PERILS	PROVIDENCES OF GOD

F. Comments

There is nothing more foolish than the transgression of God's laws.

G. A Practical Lesson

A Christian should not hold back telling others about the goodness of God to him (v. 2).

II. PSALM 108

This psalm is a combination of parts of two other psalms. A different occasion apparently called for this arrangement. Review your study of the earlier psalms (Ps. 108:1-5 and Ps. 57:7-11; Ps. 108:6-13 and Ps. 60:5-12).

III. PSALM 109

A. Title

Plea for Vengeance

B. Occasion

David was surrounded by foes who were slandering his name and returning evil for good.

C. Stanza Divisions

At verses 1, 6, 21

D. Analysis

This is the strongest of the imprecatory, or cursing, psalms. Keeping in mind that *righteous* indignation over evil is justified, observe from David's words what kind of a heart he had. What is the context of the word "praise" in verses 1 and 30?

E. Outline

1 CRY OF THE INNOCENT MAN	6 DENUNCIATION OF HIS ENEMIES	21 COMMUNION WITH HIS GOD 31

F. Comments

"The allusions to Judas (v. 8) suggests a symbolic character for the whole, and it would not be difficult to discover under the surface the lineaments of the Antichrist."[1] If the curses of verses 6-20 are spoken as a prophetic foreshadowing of just judgment on the obstinate and fixed enemies of Christ, we may profit by reading even the severest of the passages. (Cf. Matt. 26:24; 2 Thess. 1:7-9; 2:8-12).

G. A Practical Lesson

In persecution we will not find help in pitying self but in seeking the Lord.

IV. PSALM 110

A. Title

The Priest King

B. Occasion

Conspicuously a prophecy of Christ. No other psalm is quoted as often in the books of the Bible. Read Matthew 22:41-45; Mark 12:36; Luke 20:42-43; Acts 2:34-35; Hebrews 1:13; 10:12-13.

C. Stanza Divisions

At verses 1, 4

1. James M. Gray, *Christian Workers' Commentary* (Chicago: Bible Institute Colportage Assn., 1915), p. 226.

D. Analysis

Write a list of all the descriptions of Jesus that are presented in this brief but full prophetic psalm.

E. Outline

1	KING JESUS	4	PRIEST JESUS	7

F. Comments

Terrible things will be seen before the history of this world comes to an end (v. 6; cf. Rev. 9:11-21).

G. A Practical Lesson

As mighty King, Jesus takes care of our enemies; as eternal Priest He ministers for our sins.

V. PSALMS 111-118

This is the first group of hallelujah psalms in Book V. The hallelujah psalms are generally short. They are vibrant, uplifting, and optimistic; and they focus the Christian reader's spiritual eye away from himself to his glorious Lord and God.

First, read the whole group of psalms in one sitting. Then study each one individually, looking for the kinds of things you have seen in your earlier studies. Make your own title for each psalm. Be sure you see how each psalm differs from the others. Write out a list of spiritual lessons you have learned from these.

Here are some interesting facts about the psalms of this group, for background to your study:

111: An acrostic. The twenty-two lines begin with successive letters of the Hebrew alphabet.

112: A twin of Psalm 111. Also an acrostic. Compare the two in your study.

113: The first of the collection (Pss. 113-18) known as *The Egyptian Hallel* (see Ps. 114:1 for the reference to Egypt). This collection has been associated with the pilgrim festivals of the Jewish year: Passover, Pentecost, and Feast of Tabernacles.

114: Considered a lyric masterpiece. It is a song of the Exodus. (Cf. Jer. 16:14-15.)

127

115: "Psalms 115-18 were sung at the conclusion of the Passover meal, just before the worshipers returned to their homes."[2] Associate these hymns with Jesus and His apostles in the Upper Room, in connection with Jesus' last Passover.

116: Intensely personal, in contrast to the other psalms, which are mainly national.

117: Shortest chapter in the Bible. (The longest chapter is Ps. 119. Another interesting point: this is approximately the center of the Bible.) Note Paul's use of this psalm in Romans 15:8-12.

118: A processional song. Employs solos and various groups. May have been written for the occasion of the completion of the walls of Jerusalem under Nehemiah (Neh. 8:14-18). A stirring conclusion to this group of Hallel psalms.

VI. PSALM 119

A. Title

The Word of God

B. Occasion

No particular occasion is suggested.

C. Stanza Divisions

There are twenty-two stanzas of eight verses each, in this psalm. Each stanza of the Hebrew psalm has the heading of a Hebrew letter of the alphabet, with each verse in that stanza beginning with the Hebrew letter. The psalm is thus an acrostic.

D. Analysis

Practically every verse of this psalm makes reference to the Word of God, using words such as "commandment," "saying," and "judgments." Make a word study of this. Your study will include what the psalm says about God's Word. What does the psalm teach about: (1) God, (2) the psalmist, (3) persecution, (4) cause and effect, (5) the heart, (6) meditation, (7) the believer's walk, (8) in-

2. *The Wycliffe Bible Commentary,* ed. Charles F. Pfeiffer and Everett F. Harrison (Chicago: Moody, 1962), p. 538.

struction, (9) love, (10) holiness, (11) joy. List verses that would be valuable to memorize. Since Christ is the incarnate Word, how and why should He be received and obeyed?

E. Outline

There probably is no logical outline from stanza to stanza. Study each stanza as a unit by itself, and see if you detect any outline within the stanza. Pursue the suggestion that the first verse of each stanza may be a clue to the stanza's main point.

F. Comments

Psalm 19:7-9, which uses six synonyms for the word "law," may be the original seed of this large plant of the Word.

G. A Practical Lesson

"Thy word have I hid in mine heart, that I might not sin against thee" (Ps. 119:11).

Lesson 10
Psalms 120-134

These psalms are a miniature psalter in themselves, presenting a variety of themes such as are found in the entire book of Psalms. The general title given to each of the psalms is "Song of Degrees" or "Song of Ascents" (ASV). Various theories have been offered to explain the origin of this title. The most widely accepted one is that these were hymns used by the worshipers going up to the Temple on Mount Zion at the annual religious festivals (cf. Lev. 23).

It is not necessary to know the exact background of the original writing of each of the psalms in order to obtain all that God wants the reader to have. If that were the case, the authors would have incorporated these facts, under the inspiration of the Holy Spirit, into the text itself, and they would thus have been preserved through the centuries.

You will find your study of these psalms to be exhilarating. There is something about them that lifts the heart. Worship of God is prominent throughout. In your study pray that the Lord will open the eyes of your heart to behold all the treasures of this heavenly storehouse.

I. ANALYSIS

Keep pencil in hand, as you read each psalm. Underline phrases or entire verses that appear especially noteworthy. Record on the accompanying chart your own title for the psalm and the main points it presents. The first verses of some of the psalms are clues to titles for those psalms. Do the study entitled *Progression* at the end of your analysis. See if you can observe a movement onward and upward with respect to the themes of the psalms.

SONGS OF ASCENTS

PSALM	TITLE	MAIN POINTS	PROGRESSION
120			
121			
122			
123			
124			
125			
126			
127			
128			
129			
130			
131			
132			
133			
134			

Compare your titles with the following:[1]

   120 Sojourn of the Pilgrims
   121 Helper of the Pilgrims
   122 City of the Pilgrims
   123 Plea of the Pilgrims
   124 Deliverer of the Pilgrims
   125 Security of the Pilgrims
   126 Restoration of the Pilgrims
   127 Dependence of the Pilgrims
   128 Homelife of the Pilgrims
   129 Plea of Suffering Israel
   130 Redeemer of the Pilgrims
   131 Composure of the Pilgrims
   132 Assurance of the Pilgrims
   133 Brotherhood of the Pilgrims
   134 Benediction upon the Pilgrims

Note how the last short psalm is a fitting conclusion to this group.

II. NOTES

A. Psalm 120

The psalmist likens those with whom he dwelt to the people of Mesech and Kedar, who were particularly savage and warlike. The first step on this ladder of ascents is a desire to be delivered from sin and from the company of sinners and to have the peace of God.

B. Psalm 121

Study how the psalmist uses such words as "help," "keepeth," and "preserve."

C. Psalm 122

You are probably familiar with the slogan "Don't send your children to church—bring them!" Compare verse 1.

---

1. *The Wycliffe Bible Commentary*, ed. Charles F. Pfeiffer and Everett F. Harrison (Chicago: Moody, 1962), pp. 541-45.

D. Psalm 123

Note the change of pronoun from "I" to "our" and "us."

E. Psalm 124

Note the different figures of speech used to denote the dangers. What are the various methods used by Satan to trap the Christian today?

F. Psalm 125

This psalm takes us another step in the ascent. It expresses full assurance for the future. Compare this psalm with the words of Isaiah 3:10-11.

G. Psalm 126

While this psalm has reference to return from the Babylonian exile, prophetically it looks forward to the blessings of an ideal restoration of the people of God in the last day.

H. Psalm 127

The key to success in this life is given by this psalm. What do you consider to be true success?

I. Psalm 128

"Fear" means reverential trust. "Walking in His ways" means entire submission to Him—obedience.

J. Psalm 129

The history of Israel continues even to this day to be one of affliction. Why?

K. Psalm 130

Here the symbol of ascent is seen in the psalm itself: from the depths of verse 1 to the heights of the glorious consummation of verse 8.

L. Psalm 131

This is "one of the shortest psalms to read, but one of the longest to learn. . . . Lowliness and humility are here seen in connection with a sanctified heart, a will subdued to the mind of God, and a hope looking to the Lord alone."[2]

M. Psalm 132

Contrast the "afflictions" (v. 1) and the "crown" (v. 18). The psalm concerns two oaths, the one made by David (vv. 1-10), the other made by the Lord (vv. 11-18).

N. Psalm 133

Much is written in the New Testament about the need for Christians to dwell together in love and unity. In this psalm unity is likened to ointment—fragrant, precious, sacred; and to dew—refreshing and enlivening. Read John 17:20-23.

O. Psalm 134

This psalm, a fitting conclusion to the Songs of Ascents, may have been sung at the close of the evening worship service.

As you conclude your study of this lesson, write out a list of the spiritual blessings that have come to you through these psalms. In what ways are you determined to be a better Christian?

---

2. C. H. Spurgeon, *The Treasury of David* (New York: Funk & Wagnalls, 1881), 7: 86.

Lesson 11
Psalms 135-150

As though we have not yet reached the pinnacle of worship in the Songs of Ascents of the previous psalms, we now see before us two glorious heights to scale. The first of these is a group of eleven intense psalms. The second is the climactic group of the entire psalter, the psalms of praise appropriately called *The Great hallel,* or *The Hallelujah Chorus* (Pss. 146-50).[1]

Due to limitations of space in this manual, a minimum of helps will be given for your study of these psalms. You should have no difficulty in discovering truths in the psalms on your own, as you use the various methods of study presented in the earlier units of the manual.

I. PSALMS 135-145

Most of these psalms are ascribed to David. Before studying each one individually, scan the group for general impressions.

The accompanying chart may serve as a place to organize some of your observations. Use the help of the stanza divisions shown. At the close of this study be sure to list vital spiritual truths taught by these psalms.

II. PSALMS 146-150

The last five psalms are songs of pure praise. Note the frequency of the phrase "Praise ye the Lord," which is the literal translation of *Hallelujah*. Each psalm begins and ends with the phrase.

Note also the *crescendo* of praise in these psalms. Various words (e.g., sing, shout) are used to indicate praise. A study of the

1. Some regard Psalm 145 as the opening psalm of the Hallel group.

word "praise" shows the following: In Psalm 146 the word occurs only in the first two verses and the last. In Psalm 147 the word "praise" occurs in verses 1, 7, 12, and 20. In Psalm 148 it occurs in eight of the verses, and in Psalm 149 in three of the verses. But in Psalm 150, where we reach the *fortissimo* of praise, the word occurs twice in every verse and in verse 1 it occurs three times. Higher, richer, louder, stronger grows the voice of praise until this magnificent chorus ends in a mighty shout from everything that hath breath.

III. ANALYSIS

The following titles are suggested for these five psalms:

Psalm 146 Praise the Lord, O My Soul
Psalm 147 Praise the Lord, O Israel
Psalm 148 Praise the Lord, All Creation
Psalm 149 Praise the Lord with a New Song
Psalm 150 Praise the Lord, Everything That Hath Breath

See what verses in each psalm justify the above titles. In your study arrive at your own titles. They might center on such topics as (1) reasons for praise (2) descriptions of God.

As you analyze these psalms, look especially for everything that is taught concerning praise. Record all your observations, and organize them under such topical headings as (1) praise by whom, (2) times and circumstances for praise, (3) the God to be praised, (4) the hindrances to praise, (5) motives behind praise. Some of these may be explicitly stated; others may only be implied. In both cases, the truths are just as real.

For a concluding study in Psalms, review the various study units that you have followed in this study guide. Then write out a list of at least ten reasons that, in your estimation, God gave this inspired portion of the Scriptures to the world.

IV. NOTES

A. Psalm 146

The psalmist calls upon others to praise the Lord, but he also calls upon his own soul to do the same!

B. Psalm 147

This psalm tells why it is good to sing praises to God. List the reasons given.

C. Psalm 148

All creation, including vegetable and animal life, is called upon to praise the Lord. What does this reveal about one aspect of praise?

D. Psalm 149

Note the reference to a "new song." Read Revelation 5:9 and 14:3. How appropriate would this song be at the second coming of the Lord?

E. PSALM 150

Of this psalm Spurgeon writes, "We have now reached the last summit of the mountain chain of Psalms. It rises high into the clear azure, and its brow is bathed in the sunlight of the eternal world of worship. It is a rapture. The poet-prophet is full of inspiration and enthusiasm. He stays not to argue, to teach, to explain; but cries with burning words, 'Praise him, Praise him, Praise ye the Lord.'"[2]

CONCLUSION

The book of Psalms reminds one of the Christian life. At the beginning two ways are presented—the way of life and the way of death. The Christian life begins when the way of life is chosen. The Christian thereupon proceeds along this pathway, receiving instruction, guidance, and exhortation. As he journeys on he encounters various vicissitudes and fortunes, meeting frequently with grief and trouble and shame and tears, yet always finding his God to be a very present help. And as he draws near to the end he sees that this pathway of God does indeed grow brighter and brighter unto the perfect day. At the end his heart and his tongue are occupied wholly with praise of his Maker, who has redeemed him and has brought him all the way. What else can he say than "HALLELUJAH!"

2. C. H. Spurgeon, *The Treasury of David* (New York: Funk & Wagnalls, 1881), 7: 449.

Praise God from Whom all blessings flow:
Praise Him, all creatures here below:
Praise Him above, ye heavenly host,
Praise Father, Son, and Holy Ghost.

PSALMS 135—145

PSALM	Stanza Divisions	Character and Works of God	Supplications	Praise
135	1-4 5-12 13-21			
136	1-3 4-9 10-26			
137	1-3 4-6 7-9			
138	1-3 4-6 7-8			
139	1-6 7-12 13-18 19-24			
140	1-5 6-11 12-13			
141	1-2 3-6 7-10			
142	1-4 5-7			
143	1-6 7-12			
144	1-4 5-8 9-11 12-15			
145	1-7 8-10 11-13 14-16 17-21			

Bibliography

SELECTED SOURCES FOR FURTHER STUDY

Alexander, Joseph A. *The Psalms Translated and Explained.* 2 vols. New York: Scribner, Armstrong, 1873.

Armerding, Carl. *Psalms in a Minor Key.* Chicago: Moody, 1973.

Bullock, C. Hassell. *An Introduction to the Old Testament Poetic Books.* Chicago: Moody, 1979.

Gaebelein, A. C. *The Book of Psalms.* New York: "Our Hope" Pubns. 1939.

Jensen, Irving L. *Jensen's Survey of the Old Testament.* Chicago: Moody, 1978.

Kirkpatrick, A. F. *The Book of Psalms.* Cambridge: U. Press, 1951.

Leslie, E. A. *The Psalms.* New York: Abingdon Cokesbury, 1949.

Leupold, Herbert C. *Exposition of the Psalms.* Columbus: Wartburg, 1959.

Maclaren, Alexander. *The Psalms.* New York: Funk & Wagnalls, 1908.

M'Caw, Leslie S. "The Psalms." In *The New Bible Dictionary*, ed. F. Davidson, Grand Rapids: Eerdmans, 1953.

Morgan, G. Campbell. *Notes on the Psalms.* Westwood, N.J.: Revell, 1947.

Perowne, J. J. Stwarrt. *The Book of Psalms.* Grand Rapids: Zondervan, 1966.

Rhodes, Arnold B. *The Book of Psalms.* Richmond: John Knox, 1960.

Schultz, Samuel J. *The Old Testament Speaks.* New York: Harper & Bros., 1960.

Scroggie, W. Graham. *Know Your Bible.* Vol. 1. London: Pickering & Inglis, 1953.

_____. *The Psalms.* Westwood, N.J.: Revell, 1965.

Spurgeon, C. H. *The Treasury of David.* New York: Funk & Wagnalls, 1881.

Unger, Merrill F., ed. *Unger's Bible Dictionary.* Chicago: Moody, 1957.

Yates, Kyle M. "The Psalms." In *The Wycliffe Bible Commentary*, ed. Charles F. Pfeiffer and Everett F. Harrison. Chicago: Moody, 1962.